To my dear
friend with gratitude
to God for all
you mean to me

Jerry Falwell

Phil. 1:6

JERRY FALWELL:

Aflame For God

JERRY FALWELL:
Aflame For God

JERRY STROBER
RUTH TOMCZAK

Thomas Nelson Publishers
Nashville / New York

Acknowledgment

A word of acknowledgment and appreciation is due Kathy Vandegriff who graciously typed the final manuscript.

All Scripture quotations are from
the King James Version of the Bible.

All rights reserved under International and Pan-American Conventions. Published in Nashville, Tennessee, by Thomas Nelson Inc., Publishers and simultaneously in Don Mills, Ontario, by Thomas Nelson & Sons (Canada) Limited. Manufactured in the United States of America.

Library of Congress Cataloging in Publication Data

Strober, Gerald S
  Jerry Falwell: Aflame for God.

  Includes index.
    1. Falwell, Jerry. 2. Baptists—Clergy—
Biography. 3. Clergy—United States—Biography.
4. Thomas Road Baptist Church. I. Tomczak, Ruth
joint author. II. Title.
BX6495.F3S8   286′.1′0924 [B]   79-16248
ISBN: 0-8407-5172-9 (Nelson)
ISBN: 0-8407-5176-1 (Falwell)
ISBN: 0-8407-5177-X (Falwell)

Contents

7/1799

Foreword

Over a quarter of a century ago, I had the privilege of preaching in a little fundamental Baptist church in Lynchburg, Virginia. It was in this church that Jerry Falwell, as a young teenager, made his profession of faith in Christ. He was baptized into the fellowship of that Bible-believing church.

From this small beginning we can trace the footsteps of a young man who has traveled a straight path in his outreach for his Savior. Sometimes it has been delayed. On other occasions it has led through some deep, dark dungeons, where light did not appear for many days. Yet out of it all, Jerry Falwell has continued in the most unusual way—looking, reaching, struggling, testing, and growing with an affection and dedication to his Lord, to reach high goals and do great exploits for the One he loves.

As a friend of Jerry Falwell—from the time he was a roommate with one of my sons in college, through the years of infrequent but timely counsel, to the present time with the worldwide ministries he has developed and is using to bring men and women to Christ—I recognize several areas of achievement that shape his character.

Jerry was a good student. In those early days while in college, it was evident to those around young Falwell that he had that innate ability to reach out and accomplish goals, while others sat and wondered where to begin.

Jerry is a devoted pastor. Upon graduation, Jerry Falwell returned to his hometown. He accepted the pastorate of a small group of people that had banded together to form what is now the Thomas Road Baptist Church. That rather inauspicious beginning could not in any way reveal the growth and outreach of the great Thomas Road Baptist Church today.

However, in those small beginnings with a mere handful of people, there was a spirit of love and aggressiveness that was evident to those people who would find their way to that first crude, unsightly meeting place. Although the equipment and facilities were very mediocre, people came. That is the test of a young man's ministry. Does he love people? Can he reach the people and bring them to him as he follows his Lord?

Jerry is committed to evangelism. All those who know Jerry know him to be a great soul winner. Perhaps he is not an evangelist in the traditional sense of a Billy Sunday, Mordecai Ham, or others of the past generation; but he is an evangelist utilizing today's modern scientific tools that he has had the wisdom, judgment, and technique to use effectively. The printed page, radio, and television have become tools in his hand; and the work speaks for itself. *The Old-Time Gospel Hour* is known throughout North America as a soul-winning, fundamental, Bible-believing ministry that stands unapologetically for the faith of our fathers.

Jerry understands the necessity of Christian education. It seems almost incredible that a young man could, in such a short time, project and develop ministries that are so far-reaching. Liberty Schools are a living testimony of his tremendous influence on the thinking in the field of leadership in Christian education. There is no doubt in my mind that Jerry Falwell, with his emphasis upon proper training of the mind and heart of young people, will develop a mighty army of working men and women in every field of endeavor—in the ministry and social life of our country, as well as in the political and economic life of this country.

Jerry is a Christian leader. You cannot listen to his

broadcast, see his telecast, or sit in his church on a week-end and not realize that here is a man who is unafraid to challenge the evil forces of our generation. His outspoken opposition to the evils of abortion-on-demand, pornography, liquor, dope, greed, and lust that are so prevalent in this country today tells you that Falwell is standing in the right place. I have observed people from all walks of life—from men high in political influence, to the housewife who still sweeps her barren floors with a broom. I find that all alike recognize that here is a man destined to lead.

Jerry is a conscientious family man. On occasions I have been with him, traveled with him, or been in meetings where he would arrive with hardly any time to freshen up before going to the pulpit. However, he always takes time to call his family, to speak to the children, and to share his day with his companion. You cannot overlook his feelings and his earnestness as a father without realizing that he also fills this position as a Christian leader should. He does not neglect his family but gives to them love, understanding, and appreciation. To put it simply, he loves his family.

May God keep his hand upon Jerry Falwell. May he meet the test of leadership, and as a good soldier of Jesus Christ, may he sound the battle cry and help the Christian people of America to realize that God is still working to bring a nation back to God.

—Dr. John W. Rawlings
Landmark Baptist Temple
Cincinnati, Ohio

JERRY FALWELL:

Aflame For God

Chapter 1

Claiming A Mountain
For God

I thank my God through Jesus Christ for you all, that your
faith is spoken of throughout the whole world (Rom. 1:8).

Snow and ice covered the "city of seven hills," Lynchburg, Virginia, on January 21, 1977. Most citizens chose to
remain in their homes, sheltered from the bitter, subfreez-
ing weather.

On nearby Candlers Mountain, faculty members and
students of Liberty Baptist College (LBC) gathered sol-
emnly. Wrapped and chilled, twenty-five hundred of them
formed a circle in eight inches of snow and ice.

Jerry Falwell began to speak. "Liberty Baptist College
is just five years old. Only the blessing of God can explain
its very existence and its phenomenal growth in so short a
time with so many obstacles. It was the divine guidance of
God that brought each one of you here. That is the only
thing that can explain how you have withstood the hardships. You have attended classes in condemned buildings
and ridden old buses around the city. You have had poor
facilities, but you have had a rich heritage. You have seen
God perform miracles in your midst. Now our very existence is being threatened. We are out in the cold. We have
absolutely no where to meet for classes in the fall."

It was a bleak day. The snow-covered mountain was
beautiful, but barren.

"Lord, we must have a miracle," Jerry prayed. "We

have no human being to whom we can turn. We want to build on this mountain, but we need two and a half million dollars to pay off existing debts before we can even begin construction here. Then we need the money to build debt-free buildings for classes in the fall.''

Millions who later heard about the bizarre prayer meeting on the frozen mountain declared that it could never be done, that even Jerry Falwell, the leader who continually believed God for great things, could not expect this feat.

But the serious, united group on the mountain made no provision for defeat. They had pioneered a college in which lack of facilities had been more than compensated for by hard work, fervency of spirit, commitment to excellence, and deep faith in God. It was a united faculty and student body that claimed the biblical promise, ''But my God shall supply all your need according to his riches in glory by Christ Jesus'' (Phil. 4:19).

Before they slowly wound their way down the mountainside that day, the group had stood in the snow for almost two hours, with the temperature eight degrees below zero, and had prayed with their leader. ''We thank you, Lord, in advance for the answer we know will come. We praise You for the classroom buildings we will have on this mountain next fall.''

That day Jerry Falwell remembered the many cities across America where few churches preach the death, burial, and resurrection of Jesus Christ. He thought of the millions overseas who need to hear the gospel. This is why he saw not a barren mountainside, but a multi-million-dollar campus, teeming with students. He heard not the voices echoing impossibility, but the prayers of thousands of young men and women who would one day from that mountaintop dedicate themselves to spreading the gospel to the world.

Within two years of that unforgettable prayer meeting, thousands of excited students are walking on the campus of Liberty Baptist College located on Liberty Mountain (the new name of Candlers Mountain). They are young people who have learned firsthand to believe God for what most men say cannot be done. These young people have a vision and are training and preparing to go out into all walks of life to minister to a world of over 4.4 billion people.

"The Miracle of Liberty Mountain" is an attestation of God's miraculous working among His people through the leadership of Jerry Falwell, a man who dared to believe God for a mountain. It is a spectacular story, but only one part of the miracle of love, hope, faith, and power that is the story of a man who is aflame for God.

Chapter 2

Twins Are Born

Lo, children are an heritage of the LORD . . . (Ps. 127:3).

In 1757, John Lynch, the son of an Irish immigrant tobacco planter who had settled in Campbell County, Virginia, established a ferry at a ford along the James River. This was the site where trails had been made by the Monacan Indians, who from early times had farmed along the river and its tributaries. By the mid-1780s, the ferry crossing was a popular place for local traders and agriculturists, and in 1786 Lynch established a community that took his name.

The town, Lynchburg, rapidly became one of the first major independent cities in what was then a predominantly agricultural region. Located in the geographical center of Virginia, Lynchburg became one of the most beautiful cities in the South, lying in the Piedmont region of rolling hills at the foot of the Blue Ridge Mountains. During the Revolution, John Lynch would hang Tories by their thumbs until they shouted three times, "Liberty forever!" Thus, the modern term "lynching," sometimes wrongly associated with the town itself, came into common speech.

Some of the great heroes of early America lived near the town. Patrick Henry and Thomas Jefferson often used Lynch's ferry on the James to reach the county seat at New London. When asked about the town, Jefferson stated, "I consider Lynchburg the most interesting spot in the state and one most entitled to generalized patronage for its industry, enterprise, and correct course." During the Civil War, Lynchburg was a Confederate stronghold. It was this town that Lee, in desperate need of supplies, tried to reach when he was forced to surrender at Appomatox Courthouse, twenty-one miles to the east.

In the period between Reconstruction and the first third of the twentieth century, Lynchburg continued to grow as a manufacturing center and to spread out along its seven hills.

Although it was impossible to predict at the time, one of the most crucial dates in the history of the town was August 11, 1933. On this day twin boys were born to Helen and Carey Falwell, who lived in a white frame house about a mile and a half west of the downtown area. One of the twins, Gene, would follow in his father's footsteps and become an aggressive, successful businessman and, along with his older brother Lewis, consolidate and add to the family's extensive commercial interests. The other twin, Jerry, would follow a far different path, one which few would have predicted during his formative years.

Carey Falwell was involved in several businesses. He owned a restaurant, a trucking concern, and for a time during the thirties he operated all of the service stations in the city. The area surrounding the Falwell home contained several large gasoline storage tanks, and the family always had to be careful to avoid setting fires in the wooded area nearby.

Carey had a reputation for being able to spot new trends in the business world. It was said of him that he could see ten years into the future. There was, however, one problem that marred his development as an important entrepreneur. He had a drinking problem, in fact, a very significant one, which would cause his premature death at age fifty-five.

Carey Falwell had very little interest in religion or the church. He loved his family very much; however, he was a hard-driving, hard-talking man who would leave the house before dawn and be asleep just after dark. The Falwell children, who also included Virginia, a bright and happy girl sixteen years older than the twins, saw little of their dad and depended heavily on their mother for guidance and affection.

Helen Falwell was one of sixteen children. She had been born on a farm in Hollywood, Virginia, near Appomattox Courthouse, and moved twenty-five miles to Lynchburg when she married Carey. Helen was a stern disciplinarian, but she was also kind, gracious, and loving. Her sons recall that she never displayed anger or impatience. "I'm sure I'm prejudiced," Gene says, "but my mother had to be the finest woman who ever lived." Helen Falwell, who had always manifested the highest moral principles, later accepted Christ in the early days of Jerry's ministry.

Gene and Jerry shared a boyhood that was common in those Depression times. They batted balls in the nearby cow pasture and roamed Candlers Mountain. The twins entered the Mountain View Elementary School together, but after the first grade Jerry's teacher recommended that he go on to the third grade; thus the boys were separated by a year throughout their public school experiences. Jerry was a diligent student. He loved to read and also spent a great deal of time listening to the radio.

When the boys were nine years old, they attended a local Sunday school, or at least their names were recorded in the class book. Their normal practice was to answer present when the roll was called and then skip out to read the funny papers at their Uncle Matthew Ferguson's house. They usually arrived back at the church just as the class was dismissed and in time for their mother to pick them up. They stopped doing even this after Carey told his wife that she was not to make the boys attend Sunday school.

By the time Jerry began the eighth grade, he had garnered a reputation as a prankster—one which would follow him as the years passed. Once, as a fifth-grader at the Mountain View School, he let a snake loose in the classroom. This was followed up at Brookville High School by capers such as tying up the physical education teacher and locking him in the school basement. Then there was the time that Jerry placed a large dead rat in Miss Cox's desk drawer.

William E. Wright, Jerry's eighth-grade teacher, was very impressed by the lad's ability in math and spelling. But interestingly enough, in light of young Falwell's future attainments, Wright had great difficulty getting Jerry to speak out in class.

Jerry's ability as a speller carried him to the state championship in his junior year, but he lost out when he couldn't spell an unfamiliar word. This defeat led him to spend the next year reading through the college edition of a dictionary.

Jerry and his classmates were often rowdy in their behavior, and Wright would load them up with math tests timed to last the entire class period. Jerry, however, would usually finish in about fifteen minutes and spend the rest of the hour reading a favorite book.

After school, Jerry and Gene would usually stop at Mrs. Burford's County Store for a cola and a bag of peanuts. Sometimes they would walk down the road about a quarter of a mile to Henrietta Whitlow's home, where the one-hundred-year-old black woman would prepare a treat for the boys and tell them stories about Civil War times.

In the evenings, Jerry and Gene would go to the Royal Cafe in Fairview Heights where most of their high school friends hung out. From there, the gang would head off for an evening of what used to be called "good old-fashioned fun." Once they took the furniture off someone's front porch and put it on the roof. Another time, at Halloween, Jerry and his friends placed crossties from the railroad tracks that passed the Falwell's house out on the street and set fire to them. The flames set the asphalt on fire, and most of the Lynchburg Fire Department was required to put out the blaze.

Jerry and his Fairview Heights pals often had fights with youngsters from other sections of the city. They developed an interesting technique for dealing with their unfriendly neighbors. The smallest of the kids, Ray, who was nicknamed "Buttercup," would stand by himself and shake his fists at the other crowd. Just when the group was ready to attack Buttercup, Jerry and his friends would come out of the nearby bushes and join in the fray. There were, however, more somber moments in Jerry's childhood.

Perhaps the bleakest day of Jerry's young life came in 1948 when his father died of a liver ailment brought on by his alcoholism. The elder Falwell had been sick for a good part of that year, and his mood had been one of constant anger and turmoil. Yet, Jerry recalls that three weeks before his death, Carey became calm, reasonable, and quite loving. At the time, the family could not understand what had brought about this change, assuming it had something to do with the increasing gravity of his illness. Years later Jerry learned that Josh Alvis, an old friend of his father's, had led Carey to Christ just before he died.

Jerry graduated from Brookville High School with a 98.6 average and was named valedictorian. Unfortunately, he was also in trouble with the school authorities for a prank; so, instead of giving the valedictory speech, he sat out his graduation under suspension.

Chapter 3

God's Call

. . . there is joy in the presence of the angels of God over one sinner that repenteth (Luke 15:10).

In the fall of 1950, seventeen-year-old Jerry entered Lynchburg College and began to take courses that would lead to a major in mechanical engineering. His plan was to transfer in his junior year to Virginia Polytechnic Institute. At Lynchburg College he was awarded the B.F. Goodrich Citation for superior grades in mathematics. He had attained the highest average in math achieved at the college that year.

Jerry's academic pursuits, however, did not keep him from enjoying himself. He used to ride around in a black and red '34 Plymouth that became the major source of transportation for his friends. Stories are still told in Lynchburg about Jerry's driving habits. Sometimes after loading up his car with a group of boys, Jerry would accelerate to sixty miles per hour and then take the steering wheel off. At that point, he would take a pair of pliers and fit them to the nut at the head of the steering column, thus keeping the car on an even keel and frightening the wits out of his friends.

At this point in his life, Jerry Falwell was following a relatively predictable path, and his friends and family assumed that after graduation from college he would join his brothers Gene and Lewis in some kind of commercial activity. However, something was about to happen that would change the course of his life and future.

For several years, Jerry's mother had set the radio in the boy's room to the local station that carried the *Old Fashioned Revival Hour,* a religious program conducted by Charles E. Fuller from the Long Beach (California) Municipal Auditorium. During the forties and fifties, Fuller was one of the most listened-to preachers in the nation. Jerry listened to Fuller on Sunday mornings rather than get up and turn the radio off. Although he never told anyone what he thought about the program, it made a deep impression on him. He felt Fuller came across as being sincere, loving, and authoritative.

Jerry's interest in what Charles E. Fuller was saying came to a head on the evening of January 20, 1952, when he and a group of his close friends, including Jim Moon and Otis Wright, went to the Park Avenue Baptist Church for the Sunday evening service. There may be more than a little truth to the suggestion that the boys went to the church that night because they had heard the congregation contained some attractive girls.

When the boys arrived at the church, the sanctuary was almost filled, and they were directed to seats in the front row. Jack Dinsbeer, a young man a few years older than Jerry, was leading the congregation in a hymn, and an attractive, auburn-haired girl named Macel Pate was playing the piano. When Rev. Paul Donnelson began to preach, Jerry immediately recognized the similarity between the pastor's words and Fuller's radio sermons. Jerry was not accustomed to going to church. He and Gene joined the Franklin Street Baptist Church when they were twelve, but neither boy took religious activities seriously. Jerry did not even own a Bible.

Preconditioned by three years of listening to Fuller, Jerry heard again that night the life-changing gospel message of the death, burial, and resurrection of Jesus Christ.

Following the service, after talking to and reading Bible verses with Garland Carey, an elderly member of the congregation, Jerry asked Jesus Christ to take over his life and become his personal Savior. Unknown to him at the moment, Jim Moon, Otis Wright, and several of his other friends had also acknowledged Christ as their Savior.

The next day Jerry bought a Bible, a Bible dictionary, and *Strong's Exhaustive Concordance*. His thirst for the Bible was insatiable. Almost immediately he became active in the young people's department and began to spend a good deal of his time at Park Avenue Baptist Church. On Sundays he would fill up his Plymouth with friends from Fairview Heights, and they would arrive at the church with arms and legs dangling out the car's windows.

Jerry was especially concerned about his friends, and he and Jack Dinsbeer would regularly go to Fairview Heights and knock on doors. In Dinsbeer's experience, most of the people who engaged in visitation adopted a bashful or defensive attitude. Jerry, however, was quite different. He would look a potential prospect in the eye and say, "Listen, we're going to church Sunday, and I'll pick you up at nine-thirty." He was direct, but his love and concern for people drew them to him. To Dinsbeer's great surprise, nearly everyone said, "All right, I'll be ready." In the first few weeks, more than twenty young men came to the church as a result of these efforts. By the end of the summer there were fifty new fellows in the church's youth department.

It wasn't long before Jerry was showing a keen interest in the attractive pianist at Park Avenue Baptist. Macel Pate came from a strong Christian home. Her dad was a deacon, and she had started going to church at a very early age. Sam Pate, Macel's father, was a builder. Her mother was an instructor at the local shoe factory where her reputation for conscientiousness was legendary. If a new employee made a mistake, Macel's mother would take the shoes home and correct them herself.

Macel and her sisters loved to help people. They sang in a girls' trio, spent much time teaching children's classes, and frequently were seen visiting the elderly and cheering up many a lonely man and woman. Once while driving past a resthome, Macel noticed a woman sitting on the porch gazing dejectedly into the distance. Although considered a shy girl, Macel stopped her car and walked over to the porch. "Hi," she smiled, "I saw you sitting here and wondered if you wouldn't mind if I sat with you for a while." The elderly woman looked at Macel with astonishment, and tears began to slowly course down her face. "Oh, I thought no one in the world cared about me. Why should you stop honey; you are so beautiful and you have so much to live for. Run on now; don't waste your time with an old woman like me." But Macel did not leave. She listened as the woman told of a lifetime of heartache and tragedy. Macel often visited the woman, and they became close friends. Macel communicated the love of Jesus Christ to her elderly friend, and it was not long before she accepted Christ.

Only two months after his conversion, Jerry made a decision concerning his life work. At a Wednesday night prayer meeting held in March at the Park Avenue Baptist Church, Jerry remembers joining with the congregation to sing;

> Jesus, Jesus, How I Trust Him,
> How I've Proved Him O'er and O'er.
> Jesus, Jesus Precious Jesus,
> O for Grace to Trust Him More

"In the few seconds it took to sing those words," he

says, "I totally surrendered my life to God. I asked Him to use my life for His glory. I gave God my talents, my desires, and my body. I asked Him to let my occupation be communicating the gospel of Jesus Christ to men and women. It happened just that simply. There was no emotion. There was no audible expression to the congregation from me. It all happened quietly, inside my heart. From that day to this, I can honestly say that all I have ever wanted is to glorify Jesus Christ through moment-by-moment acknowledgment of His lordship in my life."

The next fall Jerry enrolled at Baptist Bible College in Springfield, Missouri, to prepare to spread the gospel. The school, which had started in 1950, was mainly a training center for preachers and missionaries. It was affiliated with the Baptist Bible Fellowship, an association of several thousand independent Baptist churches in the United States.

Jerry had already completed two years at Lynchburg College, so he entered Baptist Bible College as a junior. Jim Moon, who also went from Lynchburg to the school, gives this picture of Jerry's days at Springfield: "At BBC Jerry rose to the top, even though there were people there who had been saved a much longer period. He had an unquenchable thirst for knowledge of the Bible."

As in high school, Jerry was a great sportsman, a brilliant student, and an inventive prankster. Some of the tricks he pulled at Springfield are legendary. Once he drove a motorcycle through the boys' dorm at midnight. Another time he ran a garden hose into a friend's dormitory room. After a three-hour cleanup, Jerry appeared at the door and emptied a five-gallon can of water onto the floor. He has an aggressive nature.

Don Stone, now pastor of the Ryan Road Baptist Church in Warren, Michigan, recalls his first day at Baptist

Bible College. Jerry was a senior. "Jerry was the hero of the school. You became aware of him immediately. He had incredible personality and charisma."

John Rawlings, a founder and former president of the Baptist Bible Fellowship who is now pastor of Cincinnati's Landmark Baptist Temple, first met Jerry when he came to the college to visit his sons, Herb and Harold. "We used to have rap sessions in the dorm," Rawlings recalls, "and I was greatly impressed by Jerry's attitude. He was so sure of himself. Some people might have called it cockiness, but it wasn't. It was a strong faith in God, one that does not doubt but lays hold of God's promises. It is the faith found in the lives of God's giants."

During his first year at Baptist Bible College, Jerry asked to teach a Sunday school class at the High Street Baptist Church in Springfield. He started with an enrollment of one eleven-year-old boy. For the first three or four weeks, Jerry came to the High Street Church and in a little curtained-off area taught this single pupil. After a time, the boy, who was rather self-conscious about being the only student, managed to bring a friend. This, however, did not encourage Jerry much, and he went to the Sunday school superintendent with the intention of giving up the class. The superintendent was upset and asked Jerry to return the class book. "I didn't want to give you the class when you asked," he told Jerry. "You'll never make it in the ministry. You're just not serious enough." These words stunned Jerry. "I won't give you the book," he replied. "I want to think about this matter and pray about it."

Returning to the campus, Jerry went to the dean of students and asked for the key to an empty room on the third floor of the administration building. There he prayed from 1:30 to 5:00 each afternoon, crying out to God for understanding about the failure with the class. He prayed earnestly for the class member and for the visiting boy. Every Saturday Jerry cut a path across every park, playground, and empty lot in town searching for eleven-year-old boys. He would go out to the ball fields where the young boys were and join in their games. The love of Jesus Christ reached out to those boys through Jerry. He became their best friend, someone who cared about them and saw their potential if they would be changed by the power of Jesus Christ.

By the time school was out in May, fifty-six eleven-year-old boys were enrolled in Jerry's class. All of these youngsters had professed faith in Jesus Christ, and many of their mothers and fathers had also become Christians.

Jerry learned valuable lessons from those boys. One Saturday morning Jerry arrived at the ball field a little earlier than usual. Only one boy sat on the sidelines of the field; he was dirty and unkempt and looked up with eyes filled with hate as Jerry approached him. "Come near me and I'll kill ya," he said as he bounded away.

The next week the little guy, whose name was Johnny, sat and watched as Jerry played ball with several of the boys. "Come on and field some balls with me," Jerry called to him as he walked down the field. Johnny glared at him but slowly got up and followed. They played for fifteen minutes and then sat at the sidelines. "You're pretty good," Jerry said. Johnny picked at the grass. "No, I'm not. I don't do nothin' good."

The next Sunday Johnny came to Jerry's Sunday school class with several of the boys from the ball field. He sat with clenched fists, and the defiant expression on his face revealed how he felt about life. That day Jerry told the boys about a rugged cross and cruel men who crucified a Man called Jesus. "You know, guys," he said, "Jesus could have called ten thousand angels to come and rescue

Him that day, but He didn't because love for you and me wouldn't let him." As Johnny rushed out of the class that day, he passed Jerry and said, "I might come back to hear about the ten thousand angels, but just what is love?"

That week in the empty room on the third floor a young man with a broken heart interceded for a small boy. Jerry wept for Johnny's salvation. "Dear Father," he prayed, "help me communicate Your love to Johnny. Give me wisdom to teach Your truths."

The next Saturday Jerry visited Johnny's home. He arrived just as Johnny's mother was cursing him in the front yard. Near her were a number of children whom she unlovingly referred to as "my kids," "his kids," and "our kids." Johnny was one of "his." Jerry talked to Johnny's mother about his Sunday school class. "I don't care where he goes," she told him, "but I ain't gettin' him up. Friday and Saturday nights are our partying nights. He can get himself up and go if wants to."

Johnny came to the class faithfully. No one commented about his bare feet and dirty, ragged clothes. Jerry showed interest in Johnny, and every week their friendship deepened. He confided in Jerry about his personal problems, and one Sunday gave his life to Jesus Christ. That day a boy who had never known love found it abundantly in Jesus Christ.

Jerry went into many such homes. He saw tremendous hunger and openness in people, and after pointing them to the Savior, he knew the reward of having allowed God to love people through him. God showed him the great power that was unleashed through believing prayer, and that nothing of eternal value is ever accomplished apart from prayer.

Many who knew of Jerry's hours of prayer exclaimed, "What a price!" But God was shaping him for the great works He would accomplish through him in the years ahead. Ringing through Jerry's mind were the words, "People are lost, ill, and dying. Go and take them the gospel and be willing to pay a price." Jerry Falwell learned that those things of worth begin with full commitment. What he was to accomplish for God's glory would be in direct proportion to his faith and willingness to work.

After hearing about an attendance drop in the youth group at Park Avenue Baptist Church, Jerry decided to take a year off from his studies to work there full time. He was able to rebuild the youth program, and by the spring of 1955, 250 young people regularly attended the church. Jerry's efforts were greatly aided by two close friends, Billy and Iona Lynes, who took charge of two key classes. Billy would join Jerry in visiting teenage boys. On one occasion, Jerry led him to a rough part of town where they appealed to members of a teen gang to come to Sunday services. As a result, a number of these youngsters became active in the church. Jerry had a particularly strong feeling for the Park Avenue Church, not only because he had been led to Christ there, but also because he believed it was the only church in Lynchburg capable of reaching his unsaved relatives and friends.

In the fall of 1955, Jerry returned to Springfield to complete his education. He took a weekend position teaching the college and career class at the Kansas City Baptist Temple. This meant he had a four-hundred-mile round trip each weekend, but Jerry considered this a small price to pay for the lives he was seeing transformed by Jesus Christ.

Jerry's supervisor at the Kansas City Baptist Temple was Wendell Zimmerman, a well-known minister in the Baptist Bible Fellowship. Toward the end of Jerry's senior year, Zimmerman asked him to stay on as youth pastor. Jerry had achieved remarkable success with his college class, and Zimmerman believed this was a foundation upon which a significant youth program could be built. This offer took Jerry by surprise, for even though he was about to graduate from college, he still had not clearly thought out what avenue of Christian service he wanted to enter. Then, three weeks before graduation, Zimmerman had to be gone on a Sunday and asked Jerry to preach at the morning service.

The Kansas City Baptist Temple was one of the largest churches in the Baptist Bible Fellowship, and several hundred people normally attended the Sunday worship service. This was to be Jerry's first official sermon. Just before the service, he asked God to show him that day if he was to become a minister. Jerry preached on sanctification, from Hebrews 9 and 10. It was a typical beginner's sermon, but God honored His Word and nineteen people walked down the aisle to receive Christ, including a sixty-year-old woman who was a charter member of the church. Afterwards, she came up to Jerry and said, "I have never been born again until this moment." Jerry was shocked. "I knew that this was the sign that God wanted me to be a pastor." When Zimmerman returned to Kansas City, Jerry advised him that he would have to reject his offer.

After graduation, Jerry returned to Lynchburg. Although he and Macel had become engaged while he was in college, he now tried unsuccessfully to talk Macel into immediately marrying him. His plans were to rest for a few weeks and then go to Macon, Georgia, where Billy and Iona Lynes had recently moved. They wanted him to start a new church in their community. This idea appealed to Jerry, who even in those days saw himself as a pioneer, as someone who wanted to accomplish great things for God.

During those three weeks in Lynchburg, Jerry prayed much about God's will for his life. He asked the Lord to show him where He would have him pioneer a church, and God spoke to him clearly about the need for another church in Lynchburg. Although he remembered the words of Christ, ". . . A prophet is not without honor, save in his own country . . ." (Matt. 13:57), Jerry answered God's call.

Jerry spoke to the pastor of the Park Avenue Baptist Church about God's desire to have him start a church across town. The new church would minister to an area of the city unreached by Park Avenue Church.

Some men who Jerry greatly respected advised him not to start the church in his hometown. This grieved him, and he spent two weeks in prayer. During that time God made him willing to lose even his best friends on earth in order to do what he felt the Lord wanted. Every greatly used instrument of God has paid a price; it is often this price that stands between those who live nominal Christian lives and those who know the full power of God.

Chapter 4

The Little Church On
Thomas Road

. . . upon this rock I will build my church; and the gates of
hell shall not prevail against it (Matt. 16:18).

Luther Caudill Sr., a well-known Lynchburg artist, remembers the day he went to a downtown barber shop and
met young Jerry Falwell for the first time. "He was only
twenty-two years old then, but was so fired up about a
dream he had that he fascinated us all. He spoke enthusiastically about starting a church in Lynchburg, about
his love for the city and its people, and about what he
planned to do to help folks. None of us left the shop for a
long time. I marked that day down and told myself I would
keep my eye on that boy."

That dream was realized when on Sunday, June 21,
1956, Jerry Falwell met with thirty-five adults and their
children at the Mountain View Elementary School, the
school that Jerry had attended as a boy.

At the initial worship service, the young pastor told the
people that "if God is going to bless us, we must love souls.
Only then will God enable us to win this city for Christ."

The first problem that faced the new congregation was
finding a suitable meeting place. A few days after the first
service, a local insurance agent met Dan Dunaway, one of
the thirty-five adults who had been in the first service.

Dan told the agent that the new group was looking for an
adequate building. The next day the agent was in the

Stuart Heights section of the city, an area which had been built up in the post-World War II period with small, pre-fabricated houses. It was raining quite hard, and the insur-ance agent's car stalled. As he sat making futile attempts to start the engine, he recalled his conversation with Dan Dunaway. Suddenly, he looked over to his right and noticed a little, empty thirty-five by fifty foot building. This structure had once housed the Donald Duck Bottling Company.

The agent decided he would tell Dan Dunaway about this building. He then again tried to start his car, and this time it caught immediately. When he returned to his of-fice, the agent called Dan and told him that there was a building in Stuart Heights that might be just right for the new congregation. The next day Dan and Jerry drove over and quickly decided it would be quite adequate. Later in the day they arranged for the rental.

On June 28, the new congregation held its first service in the now famous Donald Duck building, and the church was named Thomas Road Baptist Church. Those who attended that service will never forget how their shoes stuck to the floor if they stood in one place for too long— this despite the fact that Jerry, Macel, and a number of congregants had spent several days trying to wash the syrup off the floor and walls. The Donald Duck plant was large enough to hold the adults, but since it only contained one room, separate facilities had to be found for the chil-dren. Someone in the congregation had an old tent that was soon rigged up and hooked to the side of the building in lean-to fashion. The tent was filled with holes, but at least it sheltered the children from the summer sun.

These were exciting days for the young pastor. He obtained a map of the city and made a large dot at the Donald Duck site. He then drew several circles: the first covered a ten-block radius, the second extended twenty blocks, and the third and largest circle took in a three-mile area. That week he personally visited every home within the first circle.

By the end of the summer, the little bottling plant was overflowing with adults. Jerry and his deacons realized they needed more space. They were particularly concerned with housing the rapidly increasing number of children who were coming to Sunday school.

In late August they bought the Donald Duck building and the adjacent lot. At the same time, they purchased about five thousand dollars worth of building materials and went to work on a structure that would provide more space for the worship services and classrooms for the church school. Everyone pitched in. The only professional on the job was Sam Pate, Macel's father, who received the princely sum of two dollars an hour to direct his crew of amateurs. Cold weather would be coming in less than sixty days, and the workers labored feverishly to complete the building, sometimes hammering away until late at night. One midnight, neighbors in a nearby housing development became so incensed that they called the police who gently asked Jerry and his gang to take a breather.

Although the Falwell family had been involved in the construction business, this was Jerry's introduction to the practical aspects of building. He learned to stud up walls and put on roofs, training which would have important practical implications over the years as the church continued to outgrow structure after structure.

After thirteen weeks the building was completed. It was very simple, but for the moment it accommodated the ever-increasing membership. By the end of the next spring, another sixty-foot section was added; the church now resembled a long warehouse. On June 23, 1957, 864 people attended the first anniversary service. In September of that year, the cornerstone was laid for an education building that was dedicated the following April. But this was only the beginning. The next few years were marked by incredibly rapid growth in both church membership and Sunday school attendance. Several new buildings were also constructed during this period.

It was evident to those who came in contact with Jerry Falwell that his top priority was people. He was lovingly called "Jerry" by young and old alike, a practice that continues to this day. Many who were with him during those early years remember seeing him in the streets, ministering to whomever he saw.

"I have seen him give away the shoes on his feet to a beggar who asked for them," said one elderly charter member. "He would visit widows, and after he left, each would find a twenty-dollar bill in her Bible. Jerry kept only enough of his small salary for bare essentials. There seemed to be no end to his giving—monetarily, and most importantly of himself."

One young Lynchburg salesman accepted Jesus Christ after seeing Jerry give away his new overcoat to an old man. He recalls, "I watched Jerry Falwell standing in the rain talking to an old man. He took off his overcoat and helped the man into it. Then he slipped his arm around the old guy, and I watched as he took all the money he had in his pocket and put it in the old fellow's hand. Soon he was off, walking up the road in the pouring rain. That was enough to convince me there had to be something to Christianity."

On April 12, 1958, a beautiful woman in white walked down a church aisle to a young man who loved her deeply.

There were tears in their eyes as Jerry and Macel became husband and wife in the sight of God and man.

Macel had been church pianist on the first Sunday of the Thomas Road Baptist Church and continues in that role today. During the early years of the church she worked in a local bank. It was well she did because Jerry, who was pastor, janitor, and handyman, earned only eighty-five dollars a week.

Thomas Road Baptist Church, which less than two years before had been "the little church on Thomas Road," was now well on its way to becoming one of the largest churches in the United States.

Chapter 5

Days Of Victory

And believers were the more added to the Lord, multitudes both of men and women (Acts 5:14).

Reaching out to meet the needs of people took precedence in Jerry's life and resulted in the initiation of new ministries by Thomas Road Baptist Church.

In February of 1959, Jerry, having experienced the heartache of an alcoholic father, established the Elim Home for Alcoholics on a 165-acre farm in Appomattox County. This site originally housed thirty men who met twice a day for Bible study. The men came to the farm, which was situated five miles from the nearest store and fifteen miles from the nearest dispenser of alcoholic beverages, for a sixty-day period. There they were taught a life of discipline with a Christ-centered orientation.

Time and again there was great rejoicing in the growing church on Thomas Road as the congregation witnessed lives transformed and homes put back together as a result of their church's many ministries. They were a loving, unified body of believers busy ministering to the needs of people. "How I thank God for Elim House," a man would stand and say. "If it was not for the love of Christ you showed me, I'd be spending my time in the nearest bar; my children would be out on the street instead of in the house of God, and our family would have been destroyed."

On July 20, 1962, plans were announced for the construction of a new building to be erected on Thomas Road near Perrymont Avenue. It would provide seating for eight hundred people. For the first time, the local press took notice of the economic role that the Thomas Road Baptist Church was playing in the community. On December 10, the Lynchburg *Daily Advance* commented:

> The City's sagging building industry, in the throes of a six-month slump, got a shot in the arm today with the signing of a contract between J. E. Jamerson & Sons and the Thomas Road Baptist Church.

On June 1, 1964, Jerry revealed plans for the construction of a new nineteen room education building. The two-story structure would be colonial in design to conform to the newly built sanctuary and would provide adequate space for the one thousand young people who regularly attended Sunday school. The Lynchburg Christian Academy was also established as a full-time Christian day school.

By the mid 1960s Jerry was forced to take a hard look at the church's growth rate. It had been operating with a skeletal staff that was now inadequate to meet the congregation's needs. He began a round of visits to some of the major Baptist churches in the United States. These trips convinced him of the need to find a number-two man to whom he could delegate significant responsibilities.

He remembered that a few years before, a young student from Tennessee Temple School had impressed him with his bright mind and willing spirit. This fellow, Jim Soward, joined the Thomas Road staff in May, 1967, as director of the Sunday school and music programs.

Under Jim Soward's dynamic leadership, Sunday

school enrollment grew from seven hundred in 1967 to sixty-four hundred in 1971. Knowing the value of a strong visitation effort, Jerry employed men from within the church to work twelve-hour days in an attempt to reach every household in the city with the gospel. One of these men was R. C. Worley, a man who today, at seventy-four years of age, is still visitation pastor at the church and leads hundreds of men and women to Christ each year.

Jerry was greatly concerned about the hundreds of children and their parents in Lynchburg who expressed a desire to attend the church but had no means of transportation. In 1969 Thomas Road started a bus ministry, which is today one of the largest of its kind in the nation. The church's parking lot is a busy place on Sunday mornings as bus after bus rolls in, bursting with hundreds of children, young people, and adults.

One day a friend took Jerry on what was to have been merely a leisurely boat ride up the James River. They passed a thirty-four-acre island that was connected to the city of Lynchburg by a bridge. Jerry was immediately fascinated by the beautiful little island and asked his friend who owned it. In his mind Jerry saw the island covered with boys and girls enjoying a perfect camping atmosphere. He asked his friend to circle the island several times. As they made the last circle round, Jerry bowed his head and claimed the island for God. "Jerry," his friend said, "this land is priceless, and I'm sure it is not for sale. It's kind of funny, though; when you say, 'God we need this,' watch out! A few years ago I would have bet you were crazy, but now I'm beginning to wonder if you have some special something that God likes."

That "special something" Jerry has is a deep faith in God and love for people for whom Jesus Christ died. Today thousands of children enjoy free camping at Treasure Island each summer. They come from the back streets and the ghettos, from the elite sections and middle-class homes, from near and far. In addition to a good time, they are introduced to Jesus Christ and many have their lives changed and their futures redirected.

In those early years of the church's growth, Jerry recognized the growing significance of the mass media. He had long been interested in radio. When the church was only a week old, he began a half-hour daily broadcast on WBRG, a local country and western station. Six months after the founding of Thomas Road, Jerry went on local television with a show that was aired from a studio.

During the sixties, the radio and television ministries experienced impressive growth, and by the end of the decade, Jerry was ready to move the TV program into the sanctuary, now outfitted with new color cameras.

Jerry's eyes have always been on the masses without Christ. Few but Macel know of the many nights Jerry gives to prayer after he has put in a day of intense work; these are nights of prayer for Thomas Road Baptist Church, for the city of Lynchburg, for the United States, and for the world. Jerry places maps all over the walls of the room in which he prays. He places his hand on a map of Virginia or on a map of the United States and intercedes for people. "Dear God," he prays, "touch me with a coal off the fire of Your altar. Anoint me to lead the great work You want accomplished through the Thomas Road Baptist Church. Give us a vision of a lost world, and help us in this generation to obey Your command to preach the gospel to every creature."

Jerry has never been afraid of hard work and long hours. He often says, "Jesus Christ did not give up two thousand years ago. He set His face toward the cross and refused to turn back because He knew sinful men could be redeemed no other way."

It was natural in those days for Jerry to focus on needs outside of Lynchburg. During the day he would minister in his hometown, and at night he traveled extensively within a two-hundred-mile radius of Lynchburg.

Jerry would work all day and then leave by four P.M. with Jim Soward for a meeting in another part of Virginia or another state. After Jerry would minister in the evening service of the distant church, he and Jim would return home, often driving into the early morning hours.

During those long drives Jerry would fellowship with God. He thought and prayed much about the advantages of a large church. He thought of Peter who preached his great sermon on the day of Pentecost and saw three thousand souls saved and incorporated into the first church at Jerusalem. He thought of the mandate to evangelize and how much more effectively a large church could take the gospel to the world. He knew that Thomas Road Baptist Church would never place a limitation on its growth, because the greater its manpower and finances, the better it could preach the gospel. He was thankful that the church provided a well-rounded ministry to the total needs of its congregants. As specialists in many areas were added to the staff, the church more effectively ministered to its flock. God was preparing Jerry Falwell and the church for a ministry that would soon reach worldwide. But first there were valuable lessons to learn and none sensed in those glorious days of growth that there could ever be dark days.

On Easter Sunday, 1969, ground was broken for a new three-thousand-seat sanctuary and two education buildings, the total cost of which would be over a million dollars. The Lynchburg mayor, who took part in the ceremony, announced that the auditorium would be the largest in the city. The sanctuary was opened at the end of the following June in time for the church's fourteenth anniversary service. More than ten thousand people attended Sunday school that day. Each received a copy of a book entitled *What God Hath Wrought,* which described what Jerry called, "The fourteen years of miracles which have attended this ministry in Lynchburg."

These were great days for Thomas Road Baptist Church as, Sunday after Sunday, it experienced tremendous growth. Some may have been content in a church where membership was near ten thousand, but Jerry Falwell has never rested on laurels. "There are four billion people in this world," he would repeat continually. "We must take them the life-changing gospel message."

"Hurricane Agnes continues in her path of destruction," blared reporters across the state of Virginia. "Stay in your homes. The torrential downpours and floods have made many roads impassable. We repeat—stay in your homes throughout the weekend and listen for updated reports."

Jerry Falwell listened to the news reports and issued his own announcements, while answering telephone calls from worried parishioners. "Yes, our homecoming service will go on as planned. We will not be washed out. God just will not let it happen. This is our sixteenth anniversary, and it has never rained on one of our anniversaries. It will not rain on Sunday."

Threatening clouds filled the sky Saturday evening, but Sunday, June 25, 1972, dawned brilliantly. More than nineteen thousand people filled the Lynchburg Municipal Stadium that had been rented for the big day. Five thousand folding chairs had been set up on the playing field of the sixteen-thousand-seat football stadium. Reporters from Associated Press, *Newsweek,* and many of the major Christian magazines pressed through the crowds.

At the close of the service, Jerry Falwell told of his conversion experience and wept unashamedly. More than six thousand adults knelt on the playing turf after the service and prayed that God would use their lives in a special way to take the gospel of Jesus Christ to the world.

"That was a very special day," says Macel. "The power of God evidently transformed many people. That night I could not help but pause outside Jerry's prayer chamber and listen as he prayed. "Father, thank You for the thousands of lives You touched today. Let me always see people as souls for whom Christ died. I ask for nothing but that Your life be lived out through my body. I don't want wealth for myself, but I ask for Your continual anointing on my life so I may preach the unsearchable riches of Jesus Christ. I don't want personal fame, but I ask for the strength to proclaim the matchless name of my blessed Redeemer all the days of my life. I don't want earthly power, but I ask for wisdom to declare to the world the power in the shed blood of Jesus Christ to change and transform lives."

Chapter 6

Pioneering a College

And the things that thou hast heard of me among many witnesses, the same commit thou to faithful men, who shall be able to teach others also (2 Tim. 2:2).

"I have something special to share with you tonight," Jerry told his congregation. It was a Wednesday evening in January, 1971, and the people gathered at Thomas Road wondered what their excited pastor had come up with now. They had learned that when God gave Jerry Falwell a vision, things happened.

"Turn with me to 2 Timothy 2. While He was on this earth, Jesus Christ chose twelve men to follow Him closely. Men have always been God's method for carrying the gospel to the world. Before Jesus ever preached in public He began choosing the twelve disciples. His objective was to reproduce His life in men who would bear witness of His life and carry on His work after He had returned to His Father. These twelve men shook the world for God.

"The apostle Paul knew that if his ministry was to continue after the Lord called him home, it would have to be carried on by a younger person. The Bible tells us Paul committed this responsibility to a young man named Timothy.

"Paul led Timothy to the Lord, took him on a missionary journey, and later wrote two books of instruction and admonition to him. Paul literally invested his life in young Timothy and told Timothy to invest his life in others. He said, 'Thou therefore, my son, be strong in the grace that is in Christ Jesus. And the things that thou hast heard of me among many witnesses, the same commit thou to faithful men, who shall be able to teach others also.' "

Jerry looked at his congregation. "God has been very good to us. Some of you sitting here tonight remember when there was just a handful of us. We have witnessed many miracles, and to whom much is given, much is required. Because there are four billion people living today and because of the dark spiritual condition of our world, there is a greater need for training young Timothys now than there ever has been before in history.

"Young people are the hope of our nation and our world. There are many good Christian colleges in existence today, but I do not think there are enough. I believe we have a sacred obligation to provide thousands of young people with a solid Christian education. Let us dedicate ourselves tonight to starting a college with the goal of seeing thousands of young men and women, deeply in love with the Lord Jesus Christ, who will go out in all walks of life to shake this world for God. We have the advantage of providing them with an action-oriented curriculum, training them through the framework of our local, New Testament church."

Some left church that night mumbling, "It can't be done." Others just shook their heads and smiled. They never knew what to expect from their young pastor, whose vision extended far beyond the boundaries of Lynchburg, Virgina.

Things happened quickly. By March—two months later—there was an announcement that Lynchburg Baptist College would officially open in September. It was also decided that the first year's student body would be given a free trip to Israel.

That August, 110 students arrived for their first day at the new college, which they discovered had no campus. One of those early adventurers, Steve, remembers arriving at the church where he asked, "Where is my dormitory?" He was led across the street to a little house the church had recently purchased. "Where is my room?" he asked. "Pick any room you'd like," an enthusiastic carpenter said as he fixed a hole in one wall. "But there aren't any beds," Steve said. "They're out on the porch," the carpenter called. Steve went to the porch where he found a stack of bunk beds and mattresses. "I picked out a room and set up a bed," said Steve, "and then began the most exciting, rewarding days of my life."

In His sovereignty, God led some of the finest students the college has ever had to LBC in those early years.

"I'll never forget that first year of LBC's existence," reminisces a successful pastor, "I learned more in that year than I have ever learned in my life. We had classes in the corridors of Thomas Road. I remember Jerry's saying we'd have them in the bathrooms if they were just a little bigger. There were nine guys in my room, and we had one bathroom. We had weekly shifts of times to use the shower. Some weeks my turn was at four A.M. That was bad enough, but the guy on that shift had to be the first to turn on the light and scatter what seemed like one-hundred cockroaches. We had gym classes in the parking lot of the church.

"Oh, I laugh about all that now and look back and know I wouldn't trade those days for anything in the world. We learned to value what was important in life and establish priorities. A lot of us realized how spoiled we were. We learned not to be quitters and complainers. I don't think I will ever see such a united and God-fearing student body as we were. Jerry kept chapels 'hot' and we soon caught his vision to win the world for Jesus Christ. We would often go to Jerry's home in those early days. We had great fun with Jerry, but most important of all, we observed a life totally sold out to Jesus Christ. I think that by the end of that first year almost every student had witnessed a drastic change in his or her life.''

An elementary school teacher says, ''When I first arrived at LBC and saw the lack of facilities, I was sure I'd never make it. I just couldn't figure out why God had led me away from a college with gorgeous facilities to LBC. It didn't take me long to find out that facilities mean nothing in the light of God's Spirit at work in a place. The main sanctuary of the church was always open those days. There was hardly ever a time when you would not find students praying there. We were a big, happy family who were taught to work hard and to believe God for great things. Our tuition was very low, and sometimes we would help get out a mailing asking people to help the college. We'd work long hours into the night, folding letters, inserting them, and licking envelopes. Jerry would work right with us, laughing and talking to us all.

''I will never forget that first year's trip to the Holy Land during spring break. We were gone ten days. We flew to Cyprus, then sailed on a Greek oceanliner, the 'Orpheus,' to Turkey, Lebanon, Syria, and finally to Israel. I came back from that trip singing 'I walked where Jesus walked,' thinking how my life had changed that year and how I could never be the same again.''

Basketball was LBC's sole sport that first year, and almost every man in the student body played. When they weren't playing officially scheduled games, Jerry would show up to join the team for a scrimmage.

By the end of the first year LBC had enrolled 305 full and part-time students. The second year of the college, 484 students enrolled. That year students began to be housed in camping shacks on Treasure Island. More than once during that school year students were flooded out of their living quarters.

Run-down buses transported the students around town to their classes. It was estimated that each student spent two hours daily riding the buses.

By the third year an old six-story hotel had been purchased in the downtown section of Lynchburg, and students were housed there. Some of the young men were housed at the Kennedy House, an abandoned local hospital. Hundreds of Thomas Road Baptist Church members opened their homes to students.

As enrollment spiraled those first years of the college's existence, it was necessary to rent any available buildings in the city in which classes could be held, including Ruffner Elementary and Timberlake Middle Schools. Both were condemned school buildings, the latter being one of the schools Jerry had attended as a boy.

In one of her Christmas letters to her family and friends, an LBC professor wrote,

> We are so cold in our classrooms that I had to stop in the middle of a lecture today and laugh at my prize pupil who was furiously taking notes with her gloves on. I stopped laughing when, after class, I went to my car to drive to the church for another lecture and found it stuck in the mud.

One day in 1972, a young man who had not decided on which college he would like to attend, arrived at LBC just after the chapel program had begun. He sat in the foyer of the church and heard snatches of a sermon Jerry was preaching to the students.

"Before the apostle Paul was converted he hated the Christian church and murdered Christians. No one excelled Paul in the business of playing havoc with the church. After Paul met the Lord on the Damascus Road, he was convinced that he was fighting against Christ, the living God. He began going in the other direction and doing so with all his heart. Paul became the greatest student of the Word of God the world has ever known. He became the most dedicated saint of the Church Age. He knew what it meant to suffer for the sake of Jesus Christ. Paul became a champion, a winner, a victor.

"Before he was put to death Paul could say, 'For I am now ready to be offered, and the time of my departure is at hand. I have fought a good fight, I have finished my course, I have kept the faith. Henceforth there is laid up for me a crown.'

"Students of Lynchburg Baptist College," Jerry challenged, "no matter what you are going to be, God wants you to be a champion. He wants you to be a victor for God's glory.

"A champion is not an individual star but one of a team who knows how to function with others. Men of God are not interested in gaining personal fame. The man of God says, 'I will be the best for God in the place where He puts me.' He learns to operate and function on a team.

"You must pay a price to be a champion. You must learn to endure hardness. Life is not a bed of roses. Opposition is part of this hardness you have to endure. You won't always have the applause of men. Satan is your archenemy. The moment you entered the family of God, Satan declared war on you. He wants to wreck you and your testimony. Learn how to resist the devil and he will flee from you. Learn that self is your enemy. Give everything you have and are to the Lord. Your time, your tithe, your talent—all are the Lord's. Satan, the world, and the flesh are all against you and want to keep you from being a champion. You have got to learn how to put your face to the wind.

"If you are going to be a champion, you must be single-minded in your training. God has a calling for you. The Christian life is a battle. A good soldier does not entangle himself with the affairs of this life. Love of money and bad morals are the two damaging influences that too often destroy and defeat the effectiveness of God's champions. A champion must fix his attention on high and holy things.

"A champion must learn to live by the rules. If you expect God's blessings upon your life, you must live by God's blueprint, His Word. God has a perfect will for every life. You are only going to be a champion if you find the will of God and do it. His blessings will automatically attend.

"Early in his Christian life, D. L. Moody heard a preacher say, 'It yet remains to be seen what God can do with one man who is wholly surrendered to the Lord.' Moody left that building saying in his own heart, 'By God's grace, I'll be that man.' Moody determined to be that man who was wholly surrendered to the Lord. He shook two continents for God in his day. I wonder what God would do with your life if you said, 'I will be a champion for Christ.' I know you would shake this world for God."

After the chapel message hundreds of students dedicated themselves to becoming champions for God. No one knew that day that God had worked mightily in the heart of a young man seated alone in the foyer who was not even able to catch all of the words of the message. He had not only made the choice of a college, but had made a decision that would change the course of his life. Earnestly he had prayed, "Lord, thank You for bringing me to LBC and for implanting in my life today the desire to be a champion for You. May I leave this school one day to shake this world for God."

There were many Steves and Mikes, Joans and Anns, who were led to LBC and left its grounds four years later, giants for God.

News of LBC spread across the United States. Comments were made that it was a "different" college. "They say the students at LBC really love people. Through Christian service assignments they minister to needy people no matter who they are."

One of the professors of Southwestern Theological Seminary in Fort Worth, Texas, decided to conduct an experiment and personally check out the comments. He flew to Lynchburg unannounced and checked into a motel. Would an LBC student associate with a down-and-outer? He would see.

An hour before the Wednesday evening church service at Thomas Road, the professor walked to the church. He had disguised himself as a bum; he was unshaven and had greased his hair and rubbed dirt over his shabby, loose-fitting clothes. Under his arm he carried an empty wine bottle in a soiled paper bag. He sat down on the steps and buried his face in his hands.

Tom Diggs, a freshman at LBC came up the steps. Tom sat down by the man and placed his arm around his shoulders. "Sir," he said with deep concern, "May I help you? What's wrong?" After talking to him several minutes, Tom opened his Bible. "We have all sinned, every man and woman on this earth," Tom told him. "A holy God cannot look on sin. That is why God's Son, Jesus Christ, became your substitute and my substitute on a cruel cross at Calvary. He shed His blood for you and for me and paid an awful price so that we could have access to God. God has given every man a free will; He will not force Himself on anyone. You must make your decision for or against Jesus Christ. Heaven is a place reserved for those who have repented of their sins and confessed Jesus Christ as their Lord and Savior. This is called the new birth."

As the man would not respond, Tom called Jerry Falwell who was just about to enter the church. Jerry talked to the man, told Tom he would talk to him again after the service, and directed them to an associate pastor. While Tom ran to get the associate pastor, the professor tried to make his getaway back to the motel to clean up for the service, but Tom caught him again and pleaded with him to accept Jesus Christ as his personal Savior.

Later the seminary professor wrote to Jerry and told him about the incident. "I left there praising the Lord that somebody in your church would have cared for that kind of man and would have made a determined effort to reach him for Christ. I want to thank you for leading a church to a place of keen concern for lost people. I have a deep respect and admiration for your ministry."

In the years since the founding of LBC in 1971, many have asked why Jerry Falwell, a man who likes things to be first class, started a college with no campus or facilities and why he encouraged young people to come to LBC in great numbers before proper accommodations could be acquired.

God often works in what men consider hopeless circumstances to show that it is He who is doing the work and accomplishing His purpose. Jerry Falwell obeyed the voice of God. There are thousands of young people who have gone out from LBC and are taking the gospel of Jesus Christ to the world. The hardships of those early days were planned by God, and it was He who called each of those early pioneers—young men and women who caught the vision and forgot the hardships and are today changing our world.

Chapter 7

Dark Days

For I am with thee, and no man shall set on thee to hurt thee: for I have much people in this city (Acts 18:10).

The story is told about a man who dreamed he was walking along the beach with the Lord. Across the sky flashed scenes from his life, and for each scene he noticed two sets of footprints in the sand. One set of footprints belonged to him and the other set to the Lord. When the last scene of his life flashed before him, he looked back at the footprints in the sand. He noticed that over the smooth and easy places of his life there were two sets of footprints, but many other times along the path of his life there was only one set of footprints. He noticed that this happened at the very lowest and saddest times in his life. This bothered him much, and he questioned the Lord about it.

"Lord, You said that once I decided to follow You, You would walk with me all the way. But I have noticed that during the most troublesome times in my life, over the rough and difficult places, there is only one set of footprints. I don't understand why in times when I needed You most, You should leave me."

The Lord replied, "My precious, precious child, I love you, and I would never, never leave you during your times of trial and suffering. It is true that when your life was easy, I walked at your side, and when the walking was hard and the paths were difficult, I knew that was the time you needed Me most. When you saw only one set of footprints, it was then that I carried you.''

On July 3, 1973, Jesus Christ picked up Thomas Road Baptist Church and carried her in His arms. It was on that day that Jerry and the church leaders were stunned to discover that a suit charging the church with fraud and deceit had been filed in the United States District Court by the Securities and Exchange Commission. The suit, which also declared the church insolvent, was scheduled to be heard before a federal judge on August 9.

By the early 1970s, Jerry's dream of a great church was being realized. To finance the expansion of the television, radio, and related ministries, the church had borrowed several million dollars from fourteen hundred people at eight percent interest. This sum was raised through the issuance of general obligation bonds. When he started this massive fund-raising drive, Jerry had become a major personality, not only in Lynchburg but throughout the American fundamentalist community. The achievements of the Thomas Road Church were widely recognized.

Perhaps because of inexperience and oversight, the stewardship department of the church failed to obtain a proper prospectus as required by federal regulations for the sale of these bonds. It was also found that the church's general ledgers had not been kept up to date. Jerry acknowledged the mistakes but was deeply grieved that the SEC could make such charges against the Thomas Road Church.

Jerry's faith never wavered during those dark days. Some forsook him and the church during this time of trouble, but most of the members stood firm and followed Jerry as he followed Christ. During that severe trial the united body of believers at Thomas Road looked to a leader who was steadfast in Christ. ''I blame myself for all of this," Jerry said from the pulpit, "but do not fear, God will see us through. He has led us through seventeen years of miracles. He will continue the good work He began on June 21, 1956. We will be refined after being tried in the fire. Let us come forth as gold, to be of greater use to God than ever before. We must never become discouraged or defeated. That would be selfishness; we have no time for self-indulgences. There is a world of four billion people waiting for us to take them the gospel of Jesus Christ."

Macel remembers those long, bleak days during the SEC scandal. Night after night she alone watched her husband intercede for the church. Jerry's heart was broken and contrite. His faith was untouched; to him God's Word was sure—there could be no other way. Thomas Road was God's church, and He would see it through. After hours of prayer, Jerry would rise and smile peacefully, more convinced than ever that God had placed His hand on Thomas Road Baptist Church in a very special way and would glorify Himself there by continuing to bring thousands to Himself through its ministries.

"We had each other during that time," says Macel. "We as a family drew closer to each other and to the Lord. There was much bad publicity and many looked at us with suspicion, but we knew the Lord was in control; we found our strength and joy in Him alone."

On the Wednesday night before the Friday court hearing, Jerry met with eighteen hundred members of the congregation of Thomas Road. He told them that in addition to its formal charges, the SEC also had asked that the church be placed in receivership. "The devil is after us," Jerry said. "God knows we have done nothing wrong. We have years of impeccable ministry behind us that we will not let Satan destroy. The victory is God's." Already donations, including a check for $500,000 from one concerned friend, had started flowing into the church. Friends from around the country were rallying to the Thomas Road cause. Before leaving the service early to meet with attorneys, Jerry urged the congregation to remain in prayer throughout the night. Then as a final exhortation he declared: "When we win this thing we are going to stand and sing the doxology. I do not think they will hold us in contempt."

On the morning of August 9, 1973, a crowd of 175 people filled the courtroom and spilled into the hallways. Minutes before the hearing began, Jerry walked in and was greeted with a standing ovation.

The SEC brought its big guns into place. Injunctions were requested forbidding the further sale of church bonds and a temporary receiver to be assigned to handle Thomas Road's business affairs until its financial condition returned to a sound basis.

The church was several million dollars in debt and in a classic bind. If the *Old-Time Gospel Hour,* its chief source of potential income, was cut off, money could not be raised to repay the bondholders, and the institution would go into bankruptcy. The very announcement of the suit had already caused uneasiness among the program's audience, and ugly rumors and falsehoods about the church had begun to circulate throughout the country.

For example, Sumner Wemp, who is today vice-president of Liberty Baptist College, had just accepted his position with the college. The same week as the hearing, he was supervising the loading of his household goods onto a moving van when he received a call from a friend who told him that Thomas Road's doors were padlocked. Wemp immediately phoned Jerry, who assured him this was not the case and urged him to come to Lynchburg. Wemp can still remember the confidence in Jerry's voice as it boomed over the telephone: "Sumner, we're going to make it!"

After an intensive trial, lawyers for the government agency agreed to withdraw the charges of "fraud and deceit" in the complaint against the church. The SEC also dropped its request for the appointment of a receiver and accepted the church's proposal that the court appoint an advisory board of five prominent Lynchburg businessmen to temporarily supervise its financial affairs. The judge declared, "So far as this court can determine, there is no evidence of any intentional wrongdoing by the Thomas Road Baptist Church." Turning to Jerry the judge commented, "Nothing has been said from the witness stand, Dr. Falwell, that in any way taints the good name of the Thomas Road Baptist Church."

By November a report from the special court-appointed committee said contributions to the church were in excess of the budgeted projection. Jerry sent the following comments to the editor of the Lynchburg *News:*

> At this Thanksgiving time, we would like to give thanks for all our dear friends in this city and state who have endeared themselves to us during this trying year. We thank God for all of you. We plan in a reciprocal way to show during the years ahead our love for you by continued, dedicated Christian service to our city, state, and nation.

In August of the following year, the Thomas Road financial situation had improved to the point that the church was able to announce a plan to pay off its outstanding debts. Jerry spoke with confidence and faith, "We are faced with the monumental task of eliminating millions of dollars of indebtedness. After every debt is paid off and we are operating in the black, we will adopt a policy of 'owe no man anything.' God has given me the assurance this day will come sooner than any human would have dreamed possible. Let us work and pray. The victory is God's.''

Looking back, Jerry says this was the church's most crucial period. The SEC crisis was a time not only of testing but also of preparation for greater service and accomplishment. The church learned that it was never to fear any opponent. Members had witnessed the fact that God is bigger than any opposition could ever be. The crisis had been an invaluable means of teaching them to have even greater faith in the One who once said, ''Lo, I am with you alway, even unto the end of the world'' (Matt. 28:20).

Jerry comments now, ''These ministries have been down through the valley of the shadow of death. Christ had to bring me to the place where I relinquished control of my total ministry and offered it to Him. I had been holding it, controlling it. Now I realize my position as a steward. During those hard days, God taught us some invaluable lessons. Financially and legally, we were beaten upon on every side. We learned how to call upon God, for He alone was able. We learned how to pray. We saw things accomplished through prayer that were absolutely impossible! I can honestly say that as far as the international outreach today is concerned, that valley was the turning point in our ministry. It has been a miracle. Spiritually it has been a transforming time, for God has taught us how to conquer through prayer. I am so glad there is no problem so big, so overwhelming, but what God is up to the task.''

Jerry speaks from personal experience when he preaches, ''You are not capable of doing the work of God any more than you are capable of living the Christian life. Christ is the only One who can live the Christian life; He is the only One who can operate His business, His home, and function in your stead in whatever He has called you to do. Sometimes it pleases God for us to fail. It isn't always the will of God for us to be successful in every venture. It is sometimes necessary for us to be outscored in an inning so that we can later win the ball game. Sometimes God has to redirect us. What seems to be defeat at the moment becomes ultimate victory, because in that defeat we learn what we need to know in order to win the whole contest, the ball game, this thing called life.

"Sometimes when we are praying and begging God for this and for that and nothing happens, it isn't because God is deaf or God doesn't love us anymore; it is because God has some things to teach us and communicate to us that will enable us, in His ultimate plan, to be just what He wants us to be. I look back and can recount some dark days and bitter experiences. They were all God's teaching plan for Jerry Falwell. You can recount those horrible and gruesome times when you thought you would die. All that time God was teaching you. God was cutting, burning away the impurities of the flesh so that eventually you could be an honorable vessel ready for the Master's use and prepared for every good work. We read a precious promise in Psalm 50:15: 'Call upon me in the day of trouble: I will deliver thee, and thou shalt glorify me.' "

Lynchburg Baptist College was just two years old when the SEC scandal occurred. It might seem unfortunate that the students had to suffer through the bad publicity the church received during those days and the constant threats that the college would be closed. But the students learned valuable, enduring lessons. One such young man was Lamarr Monneyham who came to LBC from Burlington, North Carolina. Lamarr graduated with a pastor's major and now is pastor of the Tri-City Baptist Temple in

Durham, North Carolina, a church he started. The church is just two years old and has an attendance average of two hundred each Sunday.

"As I look back now," says Lamarr, "I know God allowed me to go to Liberty Baptist College at just the time He did for very important reasons. Oh, the classroom lectures were sound, and I learned much. The action-oriented curriculum and my involvement in the Thomas Road Baptist Church have proved invaluable, but the key was not even in these. My exposure to Jerry Falwell was the key to my developing into a man God has been able to use for His glory. From Jerry Falwell I learned two profound things: determination and diplomacy.

"I will never forget the time at the heart of the SEC controversy. We were preparing to go to court. It was a critical time. My wife worked for one of the members of Thomas Road, and one morning I took her to work very early to open the office. We did not know Jerry Falwell had been using the office as a secluded place to pray and work. We found him sitting at my wife's desk using the telephone. He had been making telephone calls and praying throughout the night for the church's problems. He looked exhausted and was unshaven. I had never seen him look so bad.

"When I first saw him I was so shocked I couldn't say anything. Then, when he got off the phone, he turned around and seeing us, half smiled.

"How's it going Doctor?" I asked.

Jerry looked at me and said, "Great!"

"I almost began to weep. In his mind it really was great. His faith never failed. He used diplomacy when handling the SEC when most men would have lost their temper and ruined their ministry. He took a lot of hard knocks, but he got through that crisis. Now when I'm up to my elbows in problems and lack of funds I think about those days. I think: everything is 'great!' Determination and diplomacy, I'll never forget them.''

It's obvious that Jerry Falwell and the Thomas Road congregation believe that, no matter what the circumstances, the church of Jesus Christ is and always will be a ''victorious church.'' The words of the popular song, ''Church Triumphant,'' beautifully express the sentiment.

This old ship has been through battles before—storms and tempests and rocks on the shore. Though the hull may be battered, inside it's safe and dry. It will carry its cargo to the port in the sky.

God has always had a people. Many a foolish conqueror has made the mistake of thinking that because he had forced the church of Jesus Christ out of sight, he had stilled its voice and snuffed out its light. But God has always had a people.

The powerful current of a rushing river is not diminished because it is forced to flow underground; the purest water is the stream that bursts crystal clear into the sunlight after it has forced its way through solid rock.

There have been charlatans, who like Simon the Magician, sought to barter on the open market that power which cannot be bought or sold. But God has always had a people, men who could not be bought and women who were beyond purchase. God has always had a people.

There have been times of affluence and prosperity when the church's message has been nearly diluted into oblivion by those who sought to make it socially attractive, neatly organized and financially profitable. It has been gold-plated, draped in purple, and encrusted with jewels. It has been misrepresented, ridiculed, lauded, and scorned.

These followers of Jesus Christ have been, according to the whim of time, elevated as sacred leaders and martyred as heretics. Yet, through it all there marches on that powerful army of the meek. God's chosen people, who cannot be bought, flattered, murdered, or stilled. On through the ages they march, God's church triumphant!

Now listen children of God, it's alive! Discouraged pastor, it's His church and it's alive! Lonely missionary, sow the seed with confidence. It's alive, my brokenhearted friend. Old saint, you're not alone and forgotten; the church is alive. Busy mother, cast your cares on Jesus. It's alive, young student; you're not alone in serving the Lord. Faithful father, there's rest in the Lord and the church is alive. Cynical skeptic, you haven't killed God with your noisy unbelief, He's alive! So family of God raise your hands and praise the Lord, for the Church is still alive!*

---

*Church Triumphant," words and music by William J. and Gloria Gaither. © copyright 1973 by William J. Gaither. Used by permission.

Chapter 8
Crusading

. . . be ye steadfast, unmoveable, always abounding in the work of the Lord, forasmuch as ye know that your labor is not in vain in the Lord (1 Cor. 15:58).

When the bond programs of the Thomas Road Baptist Church were invalidated, it seemed impossible that the *Old-Time Gospel Hour* (the church's radio and TV ministry) and Lynchburg Baptist College could continue. At first the church had planned to deficit spend for approximately three years while the new schools and the national television ministry became self-supporting. In the meanwhile, plans had been to borrow the funds from friends for the mammoth enlargement. When the Securities and Exchange Commission and the federal court said they would not allow this procedure, two alternatives faced Jerry Falwell and the Thomas Road Baptist Church: cut back the ministry by closing Lynchburg Baptist College and the *Old-Time Gospel Hour* television and radio programs, or ask God for a miracle.

The easy way out would have greatly hurt and disappointed hundreds of young people, and deprived thousands more in the future of a Christian education. It also would have stopped the *Old-Time Gospel Hour* and deprived millions of television and radio friends of spiritual food and thousands more of the opportunity to hear the life-changing gospel message.

But Jerry Falwell does not choose the easy way, and the second alternative was the only option. He chose to believe God for a miracle. This meant immediately bringing every ministry out of deficit spending and into a self-supportive position. In addition, it was necessary to raise a large amount of money and eliminate indebtedness as quickly as possible. It also necessitated a commitment to making no expansion until all indebtedness was paid. Most said, "Let us be realistic; it cannot be done." Jerry said, "God's promises are sure."

In less than four months, more than two million dollars was received at Thomas Road during a time of national recession. Beginning at home, and then extending all across the United States, members and friends prayed and sacrificed.

"One chapel service shortly after the SEC conflict," recalls a youth pastor who was then an LBC student, "Dr. Falwell spoke to us earnestly about our willingness to sacrifice before we could expect friends around the United States to help us. We loved our college and believed in it. When, at the end of the service, we were challenged to each give one hundred dollars, or whatever God laid on our hearts to give to help pay off debts, we were all willing but a little fearful. Most of the students worked hard and were barely able to meet their own bills. I do not know of one student who pledged to trust God for less than the one hundred dollars. I remember students selling guitars and stereos and clothes—anything that was of value so they could help pay off debts.

"I had been saving money for years to pay for an engagement ring. It meant a lot to give up that money, but I had to give God what I had. God asked for it, and I simply gave it."

During the seven months between January 1, 1975, and

July 31, 1975, the LBC Chorale joined Jerry in a "barn-storming tour" across the United States in an effort to raise an additional $3 million in cash and pledges. They appeared before *Old-Time Gospel Hour* supporters at banquets and rallies throughout the nation. At these meetings Jerry would start off by saying, "I have made a mistake, and our testimony has been hurt. We appeal to you to help us."

"I hardly remember sleeping for a year," reminisces one chorale member, "but none of us really considered it a sacrifice. LBC was in trouble, and it was just natural that we all take a year off and hit the road. We traveled day and night, doing three and four concerts a day. We were a big happy family, praying together every day, believing God for miracles. Before every concert we met and prayed with Jerry and consecrated each concert to God. Jerry's major concern was that souls be saved and Christians strengthened through our ministry. He had no doubts that God would give us the money we needed. I loved to watch Jerry in those days. He was always reaching out to people—in lobbies of motels, in restaurants, at gas stations where we stopped.

"The education I got on the road that year from watching a man whose life is synonymous with total commitment to God is beyond compare. Jerry believed God supremely. He taught us to believe God and never question the way He works. Jerry was away from his family for days at a time and got very little sleep; yet he never complained. He would fly back to Lynchburg for Sundays and Wednesday night prayer meetings, then would immediately rejoin us. Some criticized Jerry in those days for asking for money. But we who knew him knew that he never asked for a dime for himself. He asked for us, for LBC students, who needed a Christian education."

One night during their seven-month tour, Jerry and the chorale preached and sang to two hundred people in a room in the coliseum in Seattle, Washington. It was a good concert, one that had been preceded by much prayer and resulted in many decisions for Christ. The service had, however, been slightly disturbed by a rock concert that was going on in another part of the building. After Jerry had spoken to the last concert guest, he took some of the chorale members to the site of the rock concert. He wanted them to see their mission field. There they witnessed a horrifying scene. Thousands of young men and women were lying on the floor, engaged in every filthy act imaginable. The discordant sounds were deafening. On the stage the rock star hero of thousands of American young people stood with outstretched arms in front of a cross, with psychedelic, fluorescent lights twirling around him. Those who were not engaged in some immoral act at the moment were bowing down to him. Drug-caused smoke so permeated the atmosphere that the policemen on patrol in the room had been instructed to work only thirty-minute shifts inside.

Jerry Falwell stood and looked at the young people, an age group especially dear to his heart because they are our nation's future, and tears filled his eyes. There was no rest for him that night. He felt in a small measure the tremendous weight of sin that was placed on Jesus Christ at the cross, and his heart ached.

Lynchburg Baptist College could not be allowed to die. Thousands of young people from every state and many foreign countries would prepare to turn this world upside down for Jesus Christ. Their greatest accomplishments were yet in the future. God was strengthening them through adversity and had allowed them to approach the brink of collapse so that they would trust only Him.

In just three years after the SEC conflict, Thomas Road Baptist Church was able to pay back most of its indebtedness and was operating in the black. Sound, professional financial procedures had been adopted, and the court-ordered special financial committee was disbanded. God had been the Victor. The skeptics had been silenced, and at 701 Thomas Road, the notes of a song sounded loud and clear: "To God Be the Glory."

During the 1975-76 academic year, 1,244 students enrolled at Liberty Baptist College (the college had been renamed). God was at work in the college and in all of the ministries of Thomas Road Baptist Church. As the U.S. Bicentennial year neared, Jerry prepared to once again go on the road with a team of eighty-three LBC students to present "I Love America" rallies across the United States.

The team traveled to 112 major cities during the Bicentennial. Two Greyhound-type buses, two large trucks, and a twenty-four-passenger airplane transported them from city to city.

Each rally was a dynamic presentation in song and message of the God and country theme. Excited young people sang out, "I love America!"

McCauley Rivera, an exuberant young black man, thrilled each audience with a speech honoring the men of the armed forces. His significant monologue ended, "I believe that this is the greatest nation on earth; and I am proud to serve her, to follow her flag, to defend her, and if necessary to die for her, for I love America."

"I'm just a flag-waving American," sang Robbie Hiner as the color guard marched with the flag and then held it, flapping in a breeze.

Many were stirred by the forceful message of Charles Hughes reciting the "Church Triumphant" and the fervor and devotion with which it was delivered.

The team traveled from city to city, performing before overflow crowds in coliseums and auditoriums. Hundreds each night came forward to accept Jesus Christ as Lord and Savior. Many young people dedicated themselves to a life of Christian service. Thousands who watch the *Old-Time Gospel Hour* and listen to the radio broadcasts, making possible these ministries through their prayers and financial support, flocked to the rallies to introduce themselves to Jerry and the team. The cast was often forced to give a second performance because of the thousands who could not get in for the first one. This would end after midnight when they would have to pack up and head for another city.

"Jesus is calling America—calling her back to the fold," young people sang in earnest, time and again; their message, backed by hours of prayer and sung with a deep love for America and her people, made them forget the aching feet and nights of little sleep.

Their theme was "Revival Now," and God indeed changed many hearts and lives in every city in which they sang and Jerry preached. Great results followed the "I Love America" rallies as pastors were encouraged in a fellowship hour with Jerry before each rally to dedicate themselves to preaching for revival.

Jerry's message was anointed and powerful: "All across America we are traveling with this program crying out, 'America, back to God!' Our message is 'revival is imperative.' We are very earnestly convinced that unless America has a spiritual visitation soon, we shall cease to enjoy the liberties and freedoms that we have enjoyed for two hundred years.

"This is a Christian nation and was so intended to be by our founding fathers. The United States is under the wrath of God not because of wicked and dishonest politicians, but because of a rebellious, disobedient, and sleeping church within her borders. Our country is in grave and imminent peril of losing its liberties. Revival is our only hope.

"Our founding fathers came to these United States to carve out a nation under God, one liberated from the tyranny of leaders and despots of the old country. They came so they could worship God according to the dictates of their own hearts. They came to this country for the advancement of the Christian faith.

"The psalmist David said in Psalm 33:12, 'Blessed is the nation whose God is the LORD. . . .' In Proverbs 14:34 we find that verse which says, 'Righteousness exhalteth a nation: but sin is a reproach to any people.' Right living promotes a nation to greatness; wrong living degrades a nation to decay.

"In 1681, that patriarch William Penn said, 'If you are not governed by God, you will be ruled by tyrants.' In 1752, we engraved on the Liberty Bell the words of Leviticus 25:10, '. . . Proclaim liberty throughout all the land unto all the inhabitants thereof . . . .'

"In 1776, fifty-six men signed a document called the Declaration of Independence. They pledged their fortunes, their lives, and their sacred honor to a document that four times specifically refers to the dependence of this nation upon God. In the midst of a time of confusion, while trying to write the United States Constitution, Ben Franklin stood and said: 'I have lived, sirs, a long time, and the longer I live the more convincing proofs I see of this truth, that God governs in the affairs of men. If a sparrow cannot fall to the ground without His notice, is it probable that an empire can rise without His aid?' At that moment the convention went to prayer, and henceforth, every morning before one order of business, they prayed.''

Jerry gave many examples of the religious character of America's origin, and many times he was interrupted by applause.

''What has gone wrong? What has happened to this great republic? We have forsaken the God of our fathers. The prophet Isaiah said that our sins separate us from God. The Bible is replete with stories of nations that forgot God and paid the eternal consequences.''

People listened attentively as Jerry answered the question, ''What is the state of the union tonight?'' He spoke about trends in the public schools, the entertainment world, and the media. He mentioned America's economic, political, military, energy, and religious problems.

''I would challenge you to find out how many churches in your town still believe and preach that the Bible is the absolutely infallible and verbally inspired Word of the living God. How many churches in your town still believe and preach the virgin birth of Jesus Christ, the sinless life of the Son of God, the vicarious death of Jesus on the cross, His burial, His resurrection, His ascension, His high-priestly ministry, His glorious second coming? How many churches in your town still have a kneeling altar or prayer room where sinners are invited every service to come and repent of their sins and trust Jesus Christ as their Lord and Savior?

''The Bible says there is hope for us, but there is a condition. 'If my people, which are called by my name, shall humble themselves, and pray, and seek my face, and turn from their wicked ways; then will I hear from heaven, and will forgive their sin, and will heal their land' (2 Chron. 7:14). Our country needs healing. Will you be one of a consecrated few who will bear the burden for revival and pray, 'O, God, save our nation. O, God, give us a revival. O, God, speak to our leaders'?

"The destiny of our nation awaits your answer."

Chapter 9

Let Us Rise Up And Build

Call unto me, and I will answer thee, and show thee great
and mighty things, which thou knowest not (Jer. 33:3).

It was January, 1977, and Lynchburg, Virginia, was
experiencing one of the coldest winters on record. Students of Liberty Baptist College were returning from their
Christmas break. The rumor was quickly spreading
throughout the student body that Timberlake Middle
School, a condemned school in which LBC was having
classes, was scheduled to be torn down the following
summer to make room for a new public school.

"But where will we go?" one student asked excitedly.

"They say Dr. Falwell is talking about an old warehouse down by the railroad tracks. It's the most dismal
place I've ever seen and would cost thousands of dollars
to make halfway acceptable for classes," another replied.

That day at the Timberlake classroom building site, the
furnace went out. Outside temperatures stood at seven
degrees. Students huddled in classrooms with coats and
gloves on. Long, blow-type heaters were rented. They
took much of the oxygen out of the air in the cold building,
and light-headed students were helped outside.

That night there was no rest for Jerry Falwell. He interceded throughout the night, asking God to give him wisdom in making the great and weighty decision that was

before him. "Dear Father," he prayed, "I place before You thousands of young people who You called to Liberty Baptist College and who we are training to be champions for Christ. Humanly, our situation looks hopeless, but we dare not look at anything humanly. You have continually worked miracles in our midst, and once again we look to You and place our complete trust in You."

For a while it looked as if a seminary ten miles north of Lynchburg, vacated by a special Catholic order for several years, could be rented or bought to provide a temporary campus for Liberty Baptist College. The contract, however, could not be negotiated.

Then a search was begun for rental property in the downtown area of Lynchburg that would have sufficient space to handle the growing student body. Costs made that possibility prohibitive.

Another alternative was to lease or purchase an eighty-five-year-old factory with three hundred thousand square feet of floor space. The cost of renovating the building to meet classroom needs would have been in excess of $1 million.

God seemed to slam every door shut in the effort to provide a temporary campus for Liberty Baptist College.

It became obvious to Jerry that God was driving him back to a very special mountain.

While flying in to Lynchburg from an out-of-town trip in 1972, Jerry had spotted a new development area. Just as the plane was turning for its final approach, Jerry and Bill Burruss, a longtime friend, looked out and saw Montview Farm, once the home of the deceased U.S. Senator Carter Glass.

"How would you like to have that property down there?" Bill had asked Jerry.

"We must obtain a large tract of land for future development requirements," Jerry had responded. "That is beautiful land."

Bill, who was in the real estate business had smiled and said, "Well, I've been talking to those people about selling the farm to me." A few days later the men had begun negotiations to obtain two hundred acres for the church.

Jerry eventually secured other large parcels of land in the same area, ending up with 3,500 acres in all for Thomas Road Baptist Church.

Many mornings before most people in Lynchburg were awake, Jerry would drive up the mountain and pray, claiming the land for God. The Candlers Mountain of his boyhood he renamed Liberty Mountain and prayed that God would one day allow them to build there the entire Thomas Road complex, including the college and schools, the church sanctuary, a senior citizens' housing development, and many other ministries.

Although for almost a four-year period plans had been to develop the LBC campus on Liberty Mountain, nothing had been done on the mountain because of the promise Jerry had made to God and to the ministry's friends that no building would take place until all unsecured indebtedness had been eliminated. Although unbelievable progress had been made in that direction and the bonds had been paid off, there was still some debt.

In 1976 many people across the nation "staked their claim" on Liberty Mountain and sacrificially helped toward paying off the mortgage on the property. On Sunday, July 4, at Liberty Mountain, approximately thirty-three thousand people participated in the two hundredth birthday celebration of our nation and the twentieth birthday celebration of Thomas Road Baptist Church. It was a day of great rejoicing and thanksgiving to God for years of miracles. As Jerry preached to the thousands on Liberty Mountain, he envisioned the day when they could begin building the campus that was so badly needed.

It was a great day. God had again, as on the previous nineteen anniversary celebrations, provided beautiful weather after days of continuous rainfall. It had stopped raining at midnight on Saturday night—a beautiful reminder of God's continual care of His people.

Although it had been one of the greatest days the Thomas Road Baptist Church had ever experienced, still, the mortgage that they had hoped to burn was not yet completely paid off. A thank you note appeared in the church's August/September 1976 issue of *Faith Aflame* magazine. It read:

> We at the Jerry Falwell Ministries take this opportunity to say a very sincere "thank you" to the many thousands of people who "staked their claim" on Liberty Mountain. The names of all you dear friends will be enshrined around the Liberty Bell when the campus building program is begun. Although we did not reach the total goal we had set, nevertheless, this endeavor has been in every way a victory. Just how soon we can begin building, only God knows. But one thing is for sure: if we attempt great things for God—expect great things from God—then great things will happen. Please keep uplifting us in prayer, that God will give us His wisdom as we plan for the future of Liberty Baptist College and our other related ministries. As the Apostle Paul so beautifully stated his thanks to the saints at Philippi in Philippians 1:3, so we likewise express this sentiment: "I thank my God upon every remembrance of you."

At the end of January, 1977, the unsecured indebtedness of the Thomas Road Baptist Church totaled $2.3

million. Three years earlier the total indebtedness had been approximately $16 million.

On January 21, 1977, in eight inches of snow and sub-freezing temperatures, more than twenty-five hundred LBC students and faculty members gathered on Liberty Mountain for a prayer meeting. Jerry acknowledged the fact that God knew what they needed and when. God had given him the assurance it was now God's time for LBC and their mountain. They sang the victory song, "I Want This Mountain," prayed, and claimed Liberty Mountain by faith. They asked God to enable them to eliminate all unsecured indebtedness by February 28, 1977, so that contractors could begin buildings for LBC's 1977-78 academic year.

In the month of February more than $2.5 million was received by Thomas Road Baptist Church to eliminate LBC's indebtedness. This money came in over and above operating expenses. It was evidently the miraculous working of God.

In March the long-awaited building program began on Liberty Mountain. Also during that month the Southern Association of Colleges and Schools sent a visiting team to examine Liberty Baptist College for Candidate Status in the accreditation process.

In late June LBC was granted Candidate Status. This status was based totally upon how well LBC had fulfilled its stated purpose. With the designation of this status, Liberty Baptist College became the only local church-affiliated fundamentalist-separatist liberal arts college in America with such regional approval. Now LBC had six years to achieve full accreditation by meeting certain academic requirements.

Many times during the seemingly hopeless days, Jerry

had stood in chapel and said: "God will never fail us. We believe God, and therefore we know the delay is all according to plan. If we had it all figured out we wouldn't need the Lord. We must place our total dependence upon Christ and give Him all the glory for the answer we know will come."

Suddenly, so many things for which God's people had prayed for so long happened! Thousands of students learned that God never moves too late. They saw Him make everything perfect in His own time, and they learned that God's delays had not been His denials.

Crews worked feverishly from March to September to ready the campus for a record enrollment.

In just six months a mountain had been transformed. On September 2, 1977, more than thirty-five hundred faculty, students, and friends sat in the hot sunshine atop beautiful Liberty Mountain. They looked at buildings many had predicted could never be built. Their hearts were filled with praise. Even sitting in the ninety-degree heat, they could not help but think back to the day in January when, in snow and bitter cold, they had prayed, "Lord, we must have a miracle." They had claimed the promise, "But my God shall supply all your need according to his riches in glory by Christ Jesus," and then they had thanked God for the answer they knew would come.

The answer had indeed come. Two classroom buildings were completed and others were in progress. The educational buildings contain forty-two classrooms, faculty and administrative offices, and other facilities for over two thousand students. Twelve dormitories were to be completed by Christmas.

In the heat, Jerry spoke, "The difference between mediocrity and greatness is vision. Our vision is to soon have all the schools on Liberty Mountain. We want fifty

thousand young people with burdened hearts training and
preparing to turn this nation around for Christ. We believe
God gave us Liberty Mountain for just that purpose. Jesus
is coming soon. What we do we must do quickly. God has
ordained that all men should be saved. He is not willing
that any should perish. We have the message of redemption—Jesus Christ and Him crucified. It is the will of God
that we tell the world the message He has given us.

"Nothing is too hard for God. We are standing in the
midst of a miracle. God started the work on Liberty Mountain and will continue to accomplish His purpose as we let
Him. We have determined, by God's grace, to be a great
beacon on a hill that cannot be hid. Until the trumpet
sounds, we will ever be a part of the continuing miracle,
'The Miracle of Liberty Mountain.' ''

More than four thousand people gathered on Liberty
Mountain on Sunday, May 7, 1978, for the fifth LBC
commencement, the first ever held on the mountain. The
1978 graduating class of 403 was the largest in the school's
history. Its size made it impossible to have the graduation
in the sanctuary of Thomas Road Baptist Church; so a
platform and chairs had been set up on the mountain. The
ceremony was described as a "Convocation of Champions," and there was great rejoicing.

Within two years of that unforgettable prayer meeting in
the snow, twenty-one large, modern buildings were completed or under construction on Liberty Mountain. Much
hard work and prayer had gone into this "miracle" campus.

In the two years since construction began on Liberty
Mountain, many crises have faced the Thomas Road and
Liberty Baptist Schools family. Each time they have gone
to God in believing prayer, and each time God has brought

them through. Students at LBC know how to pray and believe that God will do great things. They have fasted and prayed for miracle days and have time and again witnessed God's sending large sums of money to continue the work.

When the new college year began in 1978, more than one thousand freshmen arrived at LBC. The college's first chapel service for the new school year was conducted outdoors in a grassy field overlooking the rising campus. Many buildings that were to have been completed for the new school year were unfinished. There was no place large enough for the entire student body to meet at one time.

Jerry Falwell explained the seriousness of the situation to the thousands of students. "Our world is in trouble today. That is why you are here to train and prepare to minister in a world of more than four billion people who desperately need Jesus Christ. This summer we have experienced the constant threat of postal strikes, which has affected our offerings. The cost of our Clean Up America Campaign has been tremendous, but we could not, nor can we ever, stop proclaiming righteousness in our nation. Thus you see unfinished buildings that you desperately need. We serve a prayer-answering God. We have gathered on this mountain today for a prayer meeting. We desperately need $5 million and have come to ask God to supply that need by September 24, which I have set aside as "Miracle Day."

Students, faculty, staff, and friends divided in small circles all over the grassy field and earnestly prayed that God would answer the prayers of His people for $5 million by September 24.

Then Jerry stood in the August sun and preached a

message from the Book of Joshua. He described the people of Israel and their situation as they faced the high, strong walls of Jericho. The Thomas Road Baptist Church was facing similar obstacles.

"The Jews had come through four hundred years of bondage. God delivered them from the Red Sea by the hand of Moses, and after forty years of wandering in the wilderness, delivered them from the river Jordan by the hand of Joshua. They had come far by faith, but now, having arrived in the Promised Land, they found the walls of Jericho immovable. The inhabitants of Jericho had been reported to Joshua to be 'giants.' Everything seemed lost to the children of God. Defeat seemed imminent."

Jerry drew a parallel: "Liberty Mountain is our Promised Land. For many years we have prayed for this thirty-five hundred acres of sanctified property. After twenty-two years of miracles, we have arrived on Liberty Mountain. But now we find ourselves looking up at the high walls of bills and unfinished buildings. A miracle is needed."

The students listened attentively as their chancellor told how Joshua met the unseen Captain. The Lord assured Joshua of victory and gave him the plan for it. The Jews were told to march around the walls once a day for six days. Then, on the seventh day, they were to march around seven times. The men of war were to march up front. The seven priests with trumpets of rams' horns were to march directly behind them each day, sounding the trumpets all the way. The ark of the covenant would be carried in their midst. The congregation was to follow the ark.

Drawing an analogy between men of war and prayer warriors, Jerry called for thousands of local prayer warriors to "walk point," symbolic of those who go first into battle. He asked millions who were watching by television to do the same. He assured the prayer warriors that, as they circled the walls of impossibility, the preachers at Thomas Road would keep preaching and sounding forth the message of the gospel. He asked Christians of North America to join with him on this trek of faith and pray with them for a miracle.

On each of the six days preceding the September 24 "Miracle Day," Jerry drove along the circumference road of Liberty Mountain, an 11.3 mile trip. He began at the main entrance of the college and prayed continually as he drove. On Sunday, September 24, Jerry rose early and encircled the mountain seven times—79.1 miles—before the early church service at Thomas Road. The offering that day and from the previous six weeks totaled more than $7 million, $2 million more than what had been prayed for. People stood and wept and praised a God who loves to answer the prayers of His people.

Macel said, "Jerry never doubted that the money would come in. He knew God would meet our needs." Soloist Don Norman, who wondered if he would be able to make it through his song said, "This is the greatest answer to prayer I have ever witnessed in my life. God is the same yesterday, today, and forever. He still meets the needs of His children."

It was a miracle LBC students will never forget. They had been having chapel and large classes in a huge three-thousand-seat tent that was leased and erected on the mountain. They had hoped the gymnasium would be finished before extremely cold weather set in so that chapel could be conducted there, but the project had been halted when the structure was only half-finished due to lack of funds. The students braved extremely cold weather in the tent, never doubting that God would send the needed monies.

One Sunday in November a Christian family visited Lynchburg and was taken by Jerry on a tour of the mountain campus. They were concerned about students' using the tent in cold weather. When Jerry escorted the group to the site of the semi-completed gym, they asked what the cost would be of completing it. "Three hundred thousand dollars," Jerry answered. Later in the day, members of the family held a discussion and informed their host they had decided to underwrite the completion of the gymnasium.

On March 30, 1979, the students gathered in the completed gymnasium for a dedication service. They sang from hearts full of thanks, the songs "He lives," "How Great Thou Art," and "Amazing Grace." Jerry, declaring it a day of worship and thanksgiving, preached a message from Genesis 18:14: "Is any thing too hard for the LORD? . . . Let us never forget," he said, "that we are in the midst of a miracle. Sometimes, like a small child in a home, we lose sight of his growth. Let us never lose sight of the fact that God is magnifying Himself through miracle after miracle in our behalf. I thank God daily for every inch of Liberty Mountain, for every building, for every one of you students and faculty members."

Some day Jesus Christ will come again to a mountain. Until then the people at Thomas Road Baptist Church will go on building an entire Christian city on Liberty Mountain—God's Miracle Mountain!

Chapter 10

Liberty Baptist Schools

. . . where the Spirit of the Lord is, there is liberty
(2 Cor. 3:17).

One fall day seventy-five young men, the LBC football
varsity, sat in a classroom on the Liberty Baptist College
campus. The next day they would play their toughest
opponent, but now they listened intently to a pep talk
given, not by their coach, but the institution's founder.
" 'Let us not be weary in well-doing:' " Jerry said, " 'for
in due season we shall reap, if we faint not.' You are
unique; you comprise a first-class football team that hon-
ors the Lord. I know you'll play to win. Vince Lombardi
said, 'If winning isn't important, why do they keep score?'

"Your commitment to Christ will be reflected in your
playing. Let your priority be to live a victorious Christian
life characterized by intensity of spirit and total commitment to God, and then play the way you live. Living that
kind of life costs something. The Christian life is one that
demands hardness, courage, and endurance. If you know
these qualities in your life, you will be a champion both on
and off the field."

The next evening was a hot and humid one in central
Ohio. It had been a long day for fifty people crowded on a
yellow school bus parked outside the sports arena of a
major university in the north. They were the staff members and friends of the Thomas Road Baptist Church who

had flown from their homes in Lynchburg to watch the LBC Flames make their first foray into big-time football.

Although the Flames had not won that evening, they had played hard, managing some strong drives. It had been a night to remember. The "agony of defeat" had not affected the beautiful sight characteristic after every game the Flames play.

All over the field, the Flames, one on one with the opposing team's players, talked to members of the team that had just beaten them about each person's relationship with God. There were some eternal victories won that night.

After the final whistle had blown, the Lynchburg group had walked the short distance from the football stadium to the indoor, twelve-thousand-seat arena. They had toured the sports complex and been much impressed by its modern design and utilitarian facilities. They had then returned to the bus that was to take them back to the municipal airport for the return flight to Lynchburg.

When everyone had boarded the bus, the driver had started the engine and was ready to pull out of the parking lot when a man in the back yelled, "Wait a minute; the pastor isn't here." A quick check of the bus had found this to be true, and the motor was turned off. Someone had asked, "Where is he?" and the answer had come, "The last time I saw him, he was talking to the athletic director back in the arena." Jerry was very interested in arenas of that type since plans were being developed to build a similar facility on the LBC campus. He was making a study of similar complexes around the country, and no doubt he wanted to jot down every pertinent fact.

After almost an hour's wait, the group saw Jerry emerge from the building with a man and woman. He brought the couple to the door of the bus, leaned inside, and said: "I want you to meet my two friends. They have just received Christ as their Savior." Instantly, a wave of emotion, happiness, and relief swept through the bus. Everyone realized that what had happened was well worth waiting for. While some had been fretting about the delay, Jerry had been about the business that in essence had brought them all together.

In two days' time, millions of people would see his face on television; and daily, countless others were listening to his voice on the radio. But these great numbers, while not representing abstractions to the pastor, were at that moment beyond his reach. That night he sensed a spiritual need in two persons' lives, and he was prepared to take the time to guide them to Christ.

Jerry shook hands with his new friends, said goodnight, and climbed on the bus. With a peaceful smile lighting his face, he was ready to go home.

Jerry is a great sports enthusiast. He participated in numerous sports during high school and college days and is now one of the greatest supporters of Liberty Baptist Schools' teams. Jerry has always believed that outstanding athletic programs are a tool of evangelism, and he promotes the development of a first-class intercollegiate athletic program at Liberty Baptist College. LBC is aspiring to become an NCAA Division I athletic power in every major sport in the next few years.

Since the founding in 1971, LBC has come a long way, now competing in ten sports for men and women. The coaches of each sport are dedicated Christians and some have played on professional teams. Only five years old, the LBC wrestling team has set a new record by being a three-time national champion in the National Christian College Athletic Association (NCCAA). The track team also took the national championship in the NCCAA in 1979.

LBC's baseball team has gained recognition and respect throughout the East Coast by beating outstanding ball teams from major colleges and universities. When their coach, twenty-one-year pro veteran Al Worthington, came to coach at LBC, he said: "I have the full intention of building a national championship baseball program at LBC. I want a team of guys who are on fire for Christ and champions on the field." Al has done just that.

Not only is LBC well on its way to sports fame, Lynchburg Christian Academy is too. It is not unusual to see Jerry at its games, and of course, he is the one yelling the loudest!

Jerry has always said that young people love sports and music. All of the Liberty Baptist Schools have many musical groups that minister to people. The college alone has twelve different singing groups. Some students take a year out of their education to tour the United States and minister in local churches. Other groups minister to the elderly, to high school students, or to numerous others. A mission group travels overseas and conducts their concerts in the foreign languages of the countries they visit. In 1979 the "Youth Aflame" singing teams sang in four hundred high schools, three hundred churches, and two hundred detention homes.

Because of the LBC music ministry, enthusiastic young people have sung for U.S. presidents, for senators, congressmen, Supreme Court justices, governors, generals, members of state legislatures, and other dignitaries from every strata of society. They have sung in prisons, juvenile courts, skid rows, missions, shopping malls, service clubs, hotels, parks, sports stadiums, and at colleges and universities. God has sent young people of tremendous musical talent to LBC; but although gifted musicians and singers, they are first and foremost communicators of God's love. They are unusual young people.

In almost every service conducted at Thomas Road Baptist Church, one of the musical groups sings. The members of the team report to the Thomas Road family and tell them about their travels. Typical of the dedication of these young people are the words spoken by one young lady who sang with her team one Sunday evening at Thomas Road.

"It wasn't very long ago that we were in New York City. After our concert at a church we loaded up the bus. It was about 11:30 in the evening. Gordon Luff said he was going to take us on a little ride down Broadway to try to open our eyes to what the world is really like. We went down a street. I don't even remember the name of it. But for the first few blocks there were kids on the street dancing and talking. You could tell they were bored and didn't have anything to do or any place to go. They were probably from families that didn't care where they were or where they went. After a few blocks we came into a section that was full of homosexuals. There were all kinds of bars and discos for gays. We saw men dressed up like women, and that kind of took us back a bit, to think there were really places like that. A few more blocks we came into a different culture. It was China Town. I don't think there is one church there trying to reach those people for Christ. We turned and went over a few blocks and came to a place called The Bowery. All up and down that street there are houses that are condemned or should be condemned. Lying on the doorsteps of those houses we saw drunks who were passed out. There was a taxicab in front of us, and when we stopped for the stoplight, two drunks with empty bottles in their hands started wiping off the windshield of the taxicab. They expected the driver to give them some money for doing it. I suppose they wanted to go buy more booze with the money they got. They had ragged clothes on, and both looked as if their hair was falling out. They were really ugly to look at. I thought to myself, 'I bet those men aren't really the age that they look.' Yet, that's what booze had done to them.

"It's really hard to love those kind of people. I thought, 'Would I be willing to go out and put my arm around those people?' We spend a lot of time in high schools around the country. Most of the kids we see today are heading in that same direction. We try to show them love. We try to give them attention. We try to make friends with them. We've seen a lot of kids saved. But if we really saw those kids the way God sees them, then just like Jesus, we'd be kneeling in a garden, and we would sweat drops of blood and our hearts would burst inside. Then we'd see this world reached for Christ. Then there would be more Thomas Road Baptist Churches. They would be all over the world.

"We plan on going overseas again. We're going to go into high schools in Australia for six weeks. Another team will be going to Korea. Mr. Chung has opened up the military for us as well as the high schools. Our prayer and our desire is that God would break our hearts so that we might be able to see this world the way He does."

It is important to Jerry Falwell that he communicates a vision to young people like this young woman, young people who will dedicate themselves to excellence by receiving the finest education possible and then going to all segments of society to be radiant testimonies of the love of Jesus Christ.

It is evident that Jerry loves young people and those

things that interest them. "Years ago," he says, "I decided that if I had to make my life count for eternity, I would do as the Lord did, and as the apostle Paul did— reproduce myself in others and teach them the same reproductive principles. I think for the rest of my life the major part of my ministry will be gathering young men and women around me and reproducing in them what God has reproduced in me."

That he is doing this is evident. Of all the phenomenal aspects of Thomas Road Baptist Church's growth, perhaps the most amazing has been its development as a major educational center. In the short span of little over a decade, Jerry Falwell has led Thomas Road in the founding of a group of educational institutions that today are flourishing. Lynchburg Christian Academy is a private, fully accredited day school with grades prekindergarten through twelfth; the Liberty Bible Institute is a two-year college with a program centered on the English Bible; the Liberty Home Bible Institute is a correspondence course that is the mobile counterpart of the Liberty Bible Institute. In just three years of existence, the home study course has enrolled more than 8,300 students.

On the steps of an old home next to what had once been a furniture store in downtown Lynchburg, a man sat and wept. His beer can dropped from his hands as he bowed his head and prayed, asking Jesus Christ to take over his life. The young man who led this man to the Lord was on a lunch break. He was a student at Liberty Baptist Seminary, located in an old furniture building at Sixth and Church streets in downtown Lynchburg.

Now in its sixth year of existence, Liberty Baptist Seminary offers programs leading to the degrees of Master of Divinity in Pastoral Studies, and Master of Arts in

Christian Education, Christian Day School Administration, Christian Counseling, and Christian Business Administration. Plans have already been made to soon offer many other degrees, including doctoral degrees. Many of the seminary's graduates have become some of the foremost church leaders and builders either in the United States or one of several foreign countries. They exemplify well the seminary's motto: "Scriptural Scholarship Aflame for Christ and for Souls."

Liberty Baptist College in 1979 was in its eighth year of existence. It is a four-year liberal arts institution with programs leading to the Bachelor of Science degree in eight major areas: business administration, religion, communications, education and psychology, music, natural science and mathematics, social sciences, and television-radio-film.

The driving force behind the development of these educational institutions is Jerry Falwell, an individual who never received less than an "A" in his college career. Despite his academic ability, Jerry does not hold any advanced degrees beyond the Th.G. awarded by Baptist Bible College. He does hold an honorary Doctor of Divinity Degree from Tennessee Temple University, Chattanooga, Tennessee, and an honorary Doctor of Letters Degree from the California Graduate School of Theology, Glendale, California. Through intensive and continuous reading, study, experience, and observation, Jerry has more than made up for his lack of graduate training. He does, however, have a keen appreciation for formal education.

"There is nothing wrong with being uneducated," he says. "Mr. Moody did a pretty good job of reaching the world without a Ph.D. But I still believe that an educated servant of God, who is as equally committed to God as the uneducated man, can do a bigger and better work for the Lord.''

Jerry Falwell has always keenly perceived the trends of our society, which is daily growing farther away from the fundamentals of the Christian faith. ''With all due respect to some godly school teachers and administrators who are still holding forth in public schools against great odds,'' says Falwell, ''there is no question that the American public school system is fast decaying. Americans have the most modern physical plants and the finest facilities for educating their children and youth found anywhere in the world, yet they are failing to teach their children morality, spirituality, character, honesty, and righteousness.

''The educational philosophy of the modern world permeates the lives of our young people, and we see them controlled by a rationalistic approach where there are no absolutes, no right and wrong. Our public educational system has set its own standards and patterns of truth. It is man-centered. As a result, we live in a century of conflict and revolution. On every hand we see our society crumbling because of national decay and moral deterioration. America stands at a crossroad. Our society is sick. Americans are feeling that life has no purpose, no hope, and no future. Their children are permeated with a philosophy of education that leads to this hopelessness. Public schools are teaching children how to make a living but have failed to teach them how to live.

''A Christian education provides students with a philosophy for the whole man, the emphasis being on their spiritual, mental, physical, and social development. 'The fear of the Lord is the beginning of wisdom.' A Christian philosophy of education begins with God. He is the center of everything. Christian education encompasses all of life.''

Christian schools are increasing in the United States at a rate of three new schools a day. Statistics show that in academic performance, students of Christian schools are ahead of the national norm in all subject areas.

It is not unusual to find a new family in Lynchburg that has moved to the city for the purpose of enrolling their children in Lynchburg Christian Academy (LCA). The student body of LCA includes many children of Thomas Road Baptist Church members and owes its beginning to Jerry Falwell's fear that his young children would not receive a comprehensive Christian education.

He says, ''In 1966, Jerry Jr. was four years old. I very much wanted him to have the opportunity of Christian education. Jeannie was two years old then, and Jonathan had just entered the world. Hundreds of Christian parents in our city felt the same way I did about providing our children with a quality education. We began praying that God would enable us to establish such a ministry.''

Jerry's desire to start a Christian day school in Lynchburg became a reality largely through his alliance with A. Pierre Guillermin, an experienced school administrator who came on the Thomas Road Baptist Church staff in 1967. Guillermin had first met Jerry early in that year when he was in Lynchburg speaking at a local church. Through a mutual friend, they met for coffee and began to share their philosophies of Christian education. Guillermin was quite impressed with Jerry and his grasp of the educational process. He also felt very much at ease with him. ''It seemed like I had known Dr. Falwell for years, even though we had just met that night.''

Jerry told Guillermin of his dream to establish several

educational institutions. "Dr. Guillermin," Jerry said fervently, "if America is to remain free, we must raise up a generation of young people who will call this nation back to God and back to the principles upon which it was built. We must bring America back to God and back to greatness. We can only do it by helping young people find purpose in life in Christ."

Guillermin was immediately excited about Jerry's vision. He had hoped to one day become involved in an exciting, total Christian educational program and said that he would come to Lynchburg if there was the opportunity to build such a program from kindergarten through university level. He expected the pastor to laugh when he said this; instead Jerry heartily agreed, and the two men almost immediately began planning what would eventually become a highly significant undertaking in education.

As in all of the problems and issues Jerry tackles, he began to move almost immediately and with great haste toward realizing his goal. Guillermin was not surprised at the scope of Jerry's educational vision, but he was somewhat amazed at the speed at which Jerry wanted to move ahead.

What happened in so short a time is now history. The Liberty Baptist Schools are "miracle schools." They are the fastest growing Christian schools in the world today and are filled with young people who are committed to changing the world for Christ.

When Liberty Baptist College was founded in 1971, a television interviewer asked Jerry Falwell, "How do you expect to get young people in today's liberated society to subject themselves to such a structured life as your school offers?" The interviewer was making reference to the rules and regulations that every student in the Liberty

Baptist Schools must adhere to. An article in *Esquire* magazine referred to LBC's "Harsh Puritanism." After a number of years of existence, the fact is simply that students are standing in line to get into the Liberty Baptist Schools. They come because of the schools' stands and standards.

While striving for academic excellence, LBC is dedicated to showing Christian young people how to reach people for Christ through the framework of the local New Testament church. It is a practical school where learning is coupled with action. "Our graduates receive more than a sheepskin upon completion of the program here," Jerry says. "Liberty Baptist College provides high academic standards in an atmosphere of Christian learning with emphasis on practical application and spiritual development."

There is little question that the action-oriented curriculum of the college has added to its enormous success. Sumner Wemp, a professor in the college's division of religion, states: "Students see this is where the action is. They can put into practice what they learn and realize that it works. The college's motto describes it exactly, 'Knowledge Aflame!' "

In an address to pastors, Jerry summarized the mission of Liberty Baptist College as being dedicated to "raising up a generation of leaders who are educationally superior and whose strength of character and commitment to absolutes will be felt in key positions in all areas of our society."

"We are preparing students," says Guillermin, "to effectively assume their roles as Christians in all walks of life. We want to see their lives characterized by complete devotion to Christ and complete dependence upon the Holy Spirit for strength, direction, and growth. Our

L. to R.: Jerry; Charles Falwell, Jerry's grandfather; Gene; Dave Brown, an employee of Jerry's father.

Helen, Jerry's mother, on Mother's Day, 1971.

Carey H. Falwell, Jerry's father.

Jerry in first grade.

Jerry's graduation picture from
Baptist Bible College, 1956.

The Pastor's Sunday school class in
the Donald Duck Bottling Company
building, 1956.

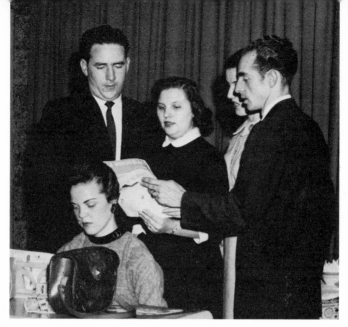

Jerry, Macel (at the piano), and three friends entertain at a Christmas party shortly after the church is started.

During the Bicentennial, Jerry Falwell and 83 Liberty Baptist College students presented "I Love America" rallies in 112 major cities.

The single most significant influence upon Jerry's ministry in recent years has been evangelist B. R. Lakin (left).

Jerry, at a Liberty Baptist
College baseball game.
Jerry has always believed
that outstanding athletic
programs are a tool of
evangelism.

The Thomas Road Baptist Church seats 3,500 people. Three Sunday morning services are needed for the congregation's adults.

L. to R.: Antoine Alexis, Sumner Wemp, Jerry, and Roscoe Brewer in Haiti where they found both spiritual and physical needs among the people.

The Liberty Baptist College campus is a miracle of God's blessing and provision.

On April 27, 1979, Senator Harry F. Byrd joined Jerry on the steps of the Capitol Building for a Clean Up America rally.

L. to R.: Jeannie, Jerry, Jonathan, Macel, and Jerry, Jr., at Wintergreen, Va.

Macel Falwell.

Jerry works while in flight to a meeting.

Jerry at the Liberty Mountain campus building site. Jerry's vision is to one day have 50,000 students training and preparing at Liberty Baptist College to go out in their generation champions for Jesus Christ.

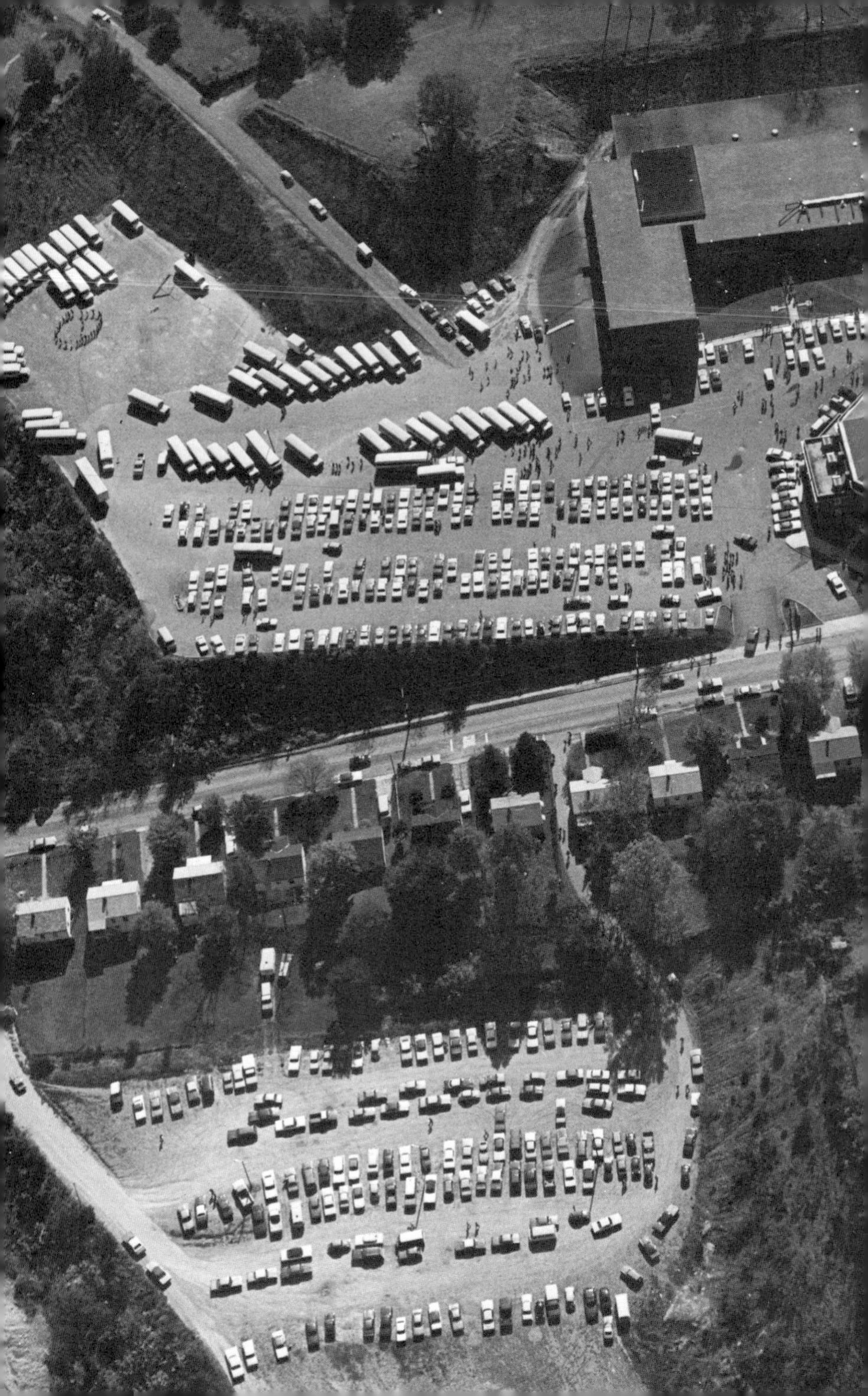

Jerry's sister, Virginia Jennings, when she worked in the church offices during the early days of the Thomas Road Baptist Church.

An aerial view of the Thomas Road Baptist Church complex.

Jerry with his twin brother, Gene.

Jerry with his mother
day he received
honorary Doctor
Divinity degree f
Tennessee Tem
Theological Semin
Chattanooga, Tennesse

Jonathan Falwell preaches his first sermon in a Junior
Church at Thomas Road Baptist Church in May 1978.

Jerry Falwell, Jr.

Jeannie Falwell

Jerry and his children on a family outing at Myrtle Beach, South Carolina, in 1974.

Jerry and his daughter, Jeannie, in the Holy Land in 1974.

Jerry's son Jonathan skiing at Wintergreen, Virginia.

The Falwell family with Paul Harvey.

Dr. Falwell confers with Israeli Prime Minister, Menachem Begin, at the invitation of the Israeli government.

Jerry with children of the Thomas Road Baptist Church during an annual children Christmas program.

Jerry relaxes at home, a rare pleasure for him.

prayer is that every student who comes to the Liberty Baptist Schools will catch a glimpse of the vision God has given Dr. Falwell and go out to make a profound impact upon this world.''

Paul Harvey, well-known radio news commentator, visited Thomas Road Baptist Church and the Liberty Baptist Schools in 1977. He made the following comments on his national news broadcast:

If you have trouble with literal interpretation of Scripture, be patient. I used to wonder whether faith to move mountains meant real mountains. Then this past rainy weekend, I saw it happening. Jerry Falwell's is a many-faceted ministry. I was particularly interested in the schools which have grown in just seven years to an enrollment of three thousand. It's mostly for the continuing expansion of those schools that in suburban Lynchburg, Virginia, a mountain is being moved. Gigantic machines are the tools, but faith is the irresistible force leveling enough of Liberty Mountain for nineteen buildings, all at once, without any government money or any borrowed money. So, the code of campus conduct and the curriculum are nobody else's business. And that means short hair, modest dresses, and no drinking or smoking anything. Even television viewing is prescribed and limited. It's the Falwell philosophy that, when you're in boot camp, you're taught to respect authority. When you get out there's time enough to learn life's lessons by trial and error, but when you attend Liberty Baptist Schools, you're taught by precept and example. There's a long waiting list of students wanting into those schools which dare to define rightness and wrongness. That waiting list is why the explosive expansion, why a mountain must be moved to make room for tomorrow.

Jerry Falwell will continue, under God, to move that mountain. These days when he drives his jeep wagon along the Liberty Mountain hillside, he envisions the day when a university with schools of law, medicine, the arts, and religion will be housed on the mountain's wooded slopes. It may happen sooner than anyone could dream possible!

Chapter 11

The Love Of A Big Man

But the fruit of the Spirit is love, joy, peace, longsuffering, gentleness, goodness, faith (Gal. 5:22).

One day a man wrote a letter to the great evangelist Billy Sunday. This man did not know the evangelist's name, but he had heard about him somewhere. He needed help badly, and in his destitute and heartbroken condition, he addressed a letter to "God's man, Adrian, Michigan." The postman immediately delivered it to Billy Sunday. There was no question in that postman's mind as to who God's man in that town was.

Jerry Falwell decided many years ago to be "God's man" in Lynchburg, Virginia. The price tag on that label has been very high. Jerry has been misunderstood by many people in his own hometown; he has been accused of being an empire builder. Speaking from experience, Jerry says, "D. L. Moody and George Mueller were, in a sense, empire builders. It all boils down to motives, not objectives. My motive is to reach people with the gospel. If your motives are right, God will bless you even when you make mistakes—and you will make mistakes a lot of times.

"I have been a Christian for twenty-seven years. When I first became a Christian I had no idea of the wonderful things God was going to do for me. Little by little God allows blessings and burdens to come into our lives. The burdens keep us humble, and the blessings make us love Him more. Sometimes we drag along. We find that His strength is made perfect in our weakness. We run along in this life looking unto Jesus, the Author and Finisher of our faith."

Jerry Falwell often speaks to the members of his congregation about living a life that is "totally sold out to the Lord Jesus Christ." He refers to Matthew 6:33, which says, "But seek ye first the kingdom of God, and his righteousness; and all these things shall be added unto you."

There is one thing that supersedes all else in Jerry's life: his heart's desire to see, in his generation, the gospel of Jesus Christ explicitly explained to every person in the world.

"When you fall in love with the Lord, having been born again through trusting the shed blood of the Savior," says Jerry, "God gives you a new heart. That new heart doesn't long for what the old heart wanted; for when a man is in Christ, he is a new creation; old things pass away."

Jerry explains what happens to the Christian who is growing in this way:

"The more you fall in love with Christ, the more love you will have for people for whom He died. When you get under the burden of seeing your friends and loved ones saved, it will keep you from sleeping some nights. It will make you fall on your face and pray for them. Souls who die without Christ will spend a conscious eternity in agony, in a real burning hell. That is what the Bible says. When you realize this, tears will flow down your cheeks. Your heart will be broken. You will want to keep Jesus first in your life so He can use you for His glory. When God loves a person through you, it will transform you. At times you will drop back into sin, but the Holy Spirit who indwells each Christian will deal with you; you will see your slovenly condition and cry out to God to cleanse you and use you again. What is your heart's desire? Is it for prestige, for power, for money, or for fellowship with God? Our existence on this earth is very short compared to eternity."

An interviewer from a prestigious magazine took a survey among members of Thomas Road Baptist Church. He asked them what was the one word they would apply to Jerry Falwell's life. He found it to be the word "loving."

John Cartwright came to Liberty Baptist Seminary after serving in the U.S. Navy. He had played football on the U.S. Naval Academy team and was a star quarterback. John is now pastor of Calvary Independent Baptist Church, a church he started in Pennsylvania. John coached football at Liberty Baptist College while preparing for the ministry at Liberty Baptist Seminary; he led the team to some great victories.

"Jerry was always our number one fan at games," he recalls. "He had more than just the interest of a chancellor. Every member of that team knew Jerry cared about him personally, aside from his being a ballplayer. There were times when I needed wisdom about a situation. Jerry was always there to help by sharing with me some of the wisdom the Lord had given him. Being around him was an education.

"When I see a mentally retarded person I think of the love Jerry has for the hundreds of those special people who Thomas Road buses in from the Training School in Lynchburg. One Sunday night Jerry came down from the pulpit after the service and began to speak to some of the mentally retarded people. They all love him. One fellow with a messy appearance came up to Jerry. He had on a dirty shirt. Jerry put his arm around him and gave him a big hug. The fellow looked up at Jerry and smiled and a tear rolled down his cheek. You never forget little things like that. It reminds me that God will love the unlovely through us if we're totally sold out to Him.''

Jerry's life has been influenced by a number of out-standing individuals. The most significant influence upon his ministry in recent years has come from evangelist B. R. Lakin. Jerry calls him ''my pastor'' and confers with him weekly. Jerry often says, ''Dr. Lakin is the greatest preacher in the pulpit today. He has remained unswervingly true to the fundamentals of the faith. His Christian conduct has been above reproach for these many years. Dr. Lakin has helped me in ways that words could never tell.''

At seventy-eight Lakin has meetings booked almost every night for the next two years. He has a deep convic-tion that God has called him to preach for as long as he has strength. That conviction stems back to a night sixty-one years ago when, in a little church at the fork of a creek, way back in the hills of West Virginia, Bascom Ray Lakin knelt at an old pine mourner's bench and trusted Christ. That night he promised the Lord, ''If you'll save me, you'll never hear the last of it.'' Lakin has been true to his word, and God has promoted him from a little church in the head of the hollow to a ministry of preaching to thousands around the world.

As Lakin stands in the pulpits of some of the greatest churches in America, he declares, ''I never expected to be any more than a country preacher. That's what I am tonight.'' Many things have changed as Lakin has preached for over half a century, things like his age, his strength, his means of transportation. But one thing has never changed. In this land or around the world his one simple message has always been: "Man is a sinner; Christ is Savior. There is a heaven to gain and a hell to shun. Life is short and eternity is long. Prepare to meet your God."

Jerry has committed his life, as has B. R. Lakin, to a ministry to people for as long as God gives him strength. He acknowledges that in himself there is nothing worthwhile, but that in Christ, with Christ producing His life in and through Jerry, there is immeasurable worth because of the tremendous price with which he was redeemed. It is no wonder that people speak of Jerry's ability to draw out the very best in those around him. Sumner Wemp says, "Jerry makes you want to rise higher than you have ever been before."

Jerry considers it a privilege to be used by God to help people. One night Jerry flew to California for a meeting. He had been up since dawn. Still, after the meeting was over, Jerry stayed, thinking that perhaps there was someone there who especially needed to talk to him. After he had talked to people for two hours, Jerry noticed that only one woman remained. She told Jerry she had driven four hundred miles to talk with him. She had been contemplating suicide all day. Today Mary Columbus is an artist on the staff of Thomas Road Baptist Church. She is a powerful influence for God.

One day as Jerry was driving down a street in Lynchburg he waved to a young man driving a beer truck. Tim Setliff was shocked.

Recalling that incident, he says, "I'll never forget that wave. I had heard about Jerry Falwell and knew enough about the church and the Bible to realize that he was doing something right, but I had seen inconsistencies in churches and preachers all my life. I even heard one preacher say one time, 'Don't ever speak to an ungodly beerman.' I tried churches but found they could not help in meeting my needs.

"Shortly before Jerry Falwell waved to me, I prayed a simple prayer to God: 'God, if you will show me one person who is real, I'll quit everything and serve you.' My whole life had been falling apart. My marriage was on the rocks. I was spending up to seventy dollars a week on booze. I would come home drunk every night. That wave was all it took. I suddenly felt, *There is a man who is real.* I finished out the week with the beer company and told the men I wouldn't be back, that I was quitting to serve the Lord. They laughed at me and told me I was crazy.

"That was the best 'crazy' thing I've ever done in my life. My wife, Mary, and I have a beautiful home now and a precious baby daughter. We have never known such peace and happiness. I am a student at Liberty Baptist College and a staff member of Thomas Road Baptist Church. My desire is to serve Jesus Christ all the days of my life."

Jerry's life revolves around people—people like Mary and Tim. He intercedes daily for the members of his church and for the students of the Liberty Baptist Schools.

McCauley Rivera and Sharon Moore were two young people who once attended Liberty Baptist College. They both had a vision of reaching people for Christ. McCauley, called "Mac" by his teachers and fellow students, was a valuable member of the "I Love America" team. He was the one who vividly portrayed a U.S. Marine and delivered a moving speech honoring the men of the armed forces.

Mac was a dynamic and aggressive young black man who was preparing to preach the gospel. His plans were well laid. After graduation he would go to Washington, D.C., to start a super-aggressive church based on all the knowledge, wisdom, and vision he had gained during his years at LBC and Thomas Road Baptist Church. He spent time in D.C., looking, praying, and planning for the proper location and building for his church.

Mac was engaged to be married to Sharon Moore, a lovely and talented junior at LBC. They shared common goals and planned to be married after Mac's graduation.

Mac had led his elder brother, Manuel, to Christ. Manuel was a student at Thomas Road Bible Institute and had plans to go to Washington to be co-pastor of the church with Mac. Another young man would be music director.

Mac and Manuel greatly loved and respected Jerry. His help and encouragement to them knew no limits. They consulted Jerry about their plans and asked him to go to Washington with them to look over the building they had found. It seemed perfect. It had a seven-hundred-seat auditorium, sound equipment, air-conditioning, and plenty of room for Sunday school classes. It even had a huge gymnasium, and Mac had visions of reaching children and teenagers through athletics.

On Thursday, February 26, 1976, Jerry flew up to Washington with Mac to view the building. As they flew to the Nation's Capital Mac asked, "Do you think there is any hope for revival among my people?" He was given a pointed answer. "Your people desperately need the gospel, as do millions of others all over the world. God will bless His Word when it is faithfully proclaimed."

They had a wonderful day. The building was all Mac and Manuel said it was. Jerry and Mac were both exuberant about the ministry in D.C. and talked excitedly all day.

They visited Mac and Manuel's mother, prayed with her, and returned to Lynchburg in the evening. On Friday night Mac preached at a little church in Lynchburg, and six people made decisions to accept Jesus Christ as their Savior.

On Saturday morning, just two days after the trip to Washington, Mac and Sharon were tragically killed by a train. People at Thomas Road were stunned. Jerry stood ashen faced and said, "God makes no mistakes." At Mount Vernon Baptist Church in Front Royal, Virginia, Jerry preached the funeral. The LBC Chorale sang. Fifteen people accepted Christ as Savior during this very touching service, and fifty young people dedicated their lives to the gospel ministry.

Mac and Sharon's vision for the city will never die. Jerry Falwell will continue to pray day and night for other precious young people to take up Mac and Sharon's mantle and go to the ends of the earth, telling people that Jesus Christ saves and transforms lives.

Another young man who was a very special part of the "I Love America" team was Charles Hughes. His heartfelt rendition of the "Church Triumphant" brought shouts of "Amen" in audiences all across the United States.

Charles was born in poverty and reared in an orphanage until he was nine years old. He was then adopted by Robert L. Hughes and his wife. Hughes is Dean of Liberty Baptist Seminary. Charles graduated from Lynchburg Christian Academy. He traveled with Jerry from time to time during his three years as a student at LBC, and on these trips Jerry would impart his vision to Charles. Charles was becoming a "fireball preacher" whom everyone loved. During his senior year at LBC he was chosen "Preacher of the Year."

After graduating from LBC, Charles enrolled in Liberty Baptist Seminary and was the first young man Jerry asked to join hands with him in the Jerry Falwell Evangelistic Association, organized for the purpose of filling hundreds of preaching engagements impossible for Jerry to meet.

Every weekend Charles and his team ministered in churches. People in all parts of the country spoke of their love for this young man who loved them and had dedicated his life to serving the Lord. People marveled that such a young man was so specially anointed by God; everywhere he went God did great things.

In March, 1978, Charles passed Jerry in the hallway of the academy building and was welcomed by a playful punch. "Jerry!" Charles spoke excitedly, "We're leaving at midnight tonight for a rally in New York tomorrow. We're expecting God to give us great results." Jerry smiled and replied, "Charles, keep lifting up Jesus. I'm praying for you and the team."

Charles kissed his wife, Kathy, goodbye that night, and he and two of his team members climbed into a bed they had fixed in the back of their van. Two of the young men laid with their heads to the rear of the van, but Charles, fearing claustrophobia, slept with his head toward the front. It was a cold night, and the closer the team got to New York, the more snow and ice they encountered. Charles, Dave, and Mark slept peacefully while Dick drove.

At 5:30 A.M. on March 17, 1978, Dick started up a hill in the northbound lane of Interstate 81 near Exit 12 at Carlisle, Pennsylvania. He passed a semitrailer climbing up the hill, cleared the top of the hill, and began his descent. It was then that the van skidded across a patch of ice and hit a guardrail. The semitrailer coming down the hill jack-knifed into the left side of the van.

The van was completely demolished, and the boys' bodies were a gruesome sight. As the rescue men worked furiously to untangle Charles, Dick, Dave, and Mark, a policeman said, "It doesn't seem possible that any of them can be alive."

Charles had been injured most severely. He had been hurled head-first against the dashboard of the van, and it was evident to all that he had massive brainstem damage. The rescuers marveled that he was still alive and wondered if he could possibly live until they got him to a nearby hospital.

Back in Lynchburg Kathy Hughes was at work at her office on Liberty Mountain at 8:40 A.M. when she received a telephone call to report to the central switchboard office. There a state police officer waited for her.

"Mrs. Hughes," he said in a grim tone. "Your husband has been involved in a serious automobile accident. You should call the Carlisle Hospital in Carlisle, Pennsylvania, at once." Kathy quietly made the call and was informed that Charles was in very critical condition. She should make arrangements to go to Carlisle immediately.

Charles's father had spent most of that week at home in bed with a fever. Now he received a telephone call telling him that Charles was severely hurt and was not expected to live. Robert and Mary Lou Hughes immediately knelt and prayed. They could not help but weep. Jerry was conducting meetings in Michigan when the news reached him. He immediately called a special prayer meeting among those who were present with him and then made arrangements to fly to Carlisle.

When the Hughes family and Jerry arrived at the hospital, they were told that Charles had less than a five percent chance to live. Charles's father told his family they must not stop praying for a miracle unless God Himself told them to stop.

Incredibly, as the days passed, Charles lived on. Dick, Dave, and Mark showed signs of improvement and were taken off the critical list and removed from the intensive care unit. Mark's recovery was miraculous. He had suffered so many broken bones that fats poured into his blood stream, and he developed a condition known as fatty embolism. This resulted in blood clots in his body and caused him to suffer from a terrible delirium. Mark's family was told that if a blood clot reached his heart he would die, and if one traveled to his brain he would be mentally retarded for the rest of his life. But God completely restored Mark's body.

Meanwhile, Charles tenaciously clung to life. None of the hospital personnel believed there was any hope for recovery. Charles had severe brain damage and multiple head injuries. His ruptured spleen was immediately removed, yet still he clung to life.

As the days passed, Charles's condition grew progressively worse. In addition to swelling of tissue around the brain, his stomach developed severe stress ulcers, causing profuse internal bleeding. The doctors believed that if he didn't die of brain damage surely he would hemorrhage to death. People all over the country continued to pray while medical experts worked feverishly to save Charles's life. Time and again, day after day, Charles went to the very brink of death. Each time God saw fit to spare his life. Doctors were frank. "We have done everything that is medically possible. All evidence points to the fact that this young man cannot possibly live."

Jerry kept a constant prayer vigil going for Charles. One

Sunday morning shortly after the accident, Robbie Hiner, a special friend of Charles's, sang on the *Old-Time Gospel Hour*. He told how he had driven to LBC in an old hearse, barefooted and full of rebellion because of his father's insistence that he attend LBC. But at school God broke his heart. Robbie told about his travels with Charles and how, night after night on the road, they stayed up half the night sharing their vision of spreading the gospel through the gifts God had given them.

After the service that morning, Jerry met Robbie in the choir room. He took him by the shoulders and said, "Robbie, I want you to know that I love you." Tears flowed down Jerry's face.

"I know you do Jerry," Robbie said, "You didn't have to say it."

"Yes, Robbie," Jerry said, "you know that, and I know Charles knew that too; but how I wish I had said those words to him more often."

That day things were very bleak in the intensive care unit in the Carlisle hospital. Charles was hemorrhaging again, and his entire family was called in.

That spring night in 1978 during the Sunday evening service of Thomas Road Baptist Church, Jerry announced that the speaker for the 1979 commencement of the Liberty Baptist Schools would be Charles Hughes. People sat stunned; many cried. Charles had been in a coma for weeks. The doctors said that if Charles miraculously did become one of the five percent who lived, he would be no more than a vegetable the rest of his life due to the massive brain damage he had sustained.

In the first seven weeks after the accident, Charles underwent seven major surgeries. He could not breathe on his own or maintain his own body temperature. As he watched his son struggle to stay alive day after day, Reverend Hughes was tempted to pray that God would take his son.

"But then," says Hughes, "I felt God telling me to wait, that His Son too had suffered, that it was His will for Charles to be raised up again. I could not think then of praying anything but that God would completely restore Charles to his wife as a strong husband and a spirit-filled man of God."

Perhaps this explains his words to a reporter who called the hospital on a day when the entire family had been called in to gather around Charles's bed at a crucial time. "They called us all to the hospital today, saying Charles has but minutes to live. But God has given me the assurance Charles will preach again."

In the critical days that followed, Charles's family refused to give up hope. They prayed continually and ministered among the hospital personnel. Thousands of calls from around the nation flooded the Carlisle hospital. "We have never seen anything like it," said a nurse. "You would think Charles was a movie star. I have never seen such great love for a young man."

Two and a half months after the accident, as pressure was relieved on Charles' swollen brain, he began to come out of the coma. One day he miraculously took his wife's hand and kissed it. He mouthed the words, "I love you." The entire hospital rejoiced. Doctors and nurses came running to the family with tears streaming down their faces. Soon Charles whispered words of thanks to Jerry and the Thomas Road Baptist Church for prayers he knew had been prayed on his behalf.

On July 9, 1978, Falwell announced to the congregation at Thomas Road and to the approximately twenty million viewers of the *Old-Time Gospel Hour* that he had a surprise for them. Jerry's lips trembled as he turned and looked at the door at the back of the choir loft. The door slowly opened, and Charles Hughes walked out supported by his father. Thousands stood and cried and applauded. All that could be said was, "To God be all the glory."

Some of Charles's doctors have said that because of what God did to restore Charles they can now believe in miracles. Just as Jerry had said by faith, Charles Hughes was the speaker at the 1979 LBC commencement ceremony.

Today, Charles attends Liberty Baptist Seminary and is preaching and telling people with all his strength that Jesus Christ is the answer to life.

Chapter 12

A Happy, Loving Family

From the beginning of the creation God made them male and female. For this cause shall a man leave his father and mother, and cleave to his wife; and they twain shall be one flesh: so then they are no more twain, but one flesh. What therefore God hath joined together, let not man put asunder (Mark 10:6-9).

It is 6:00 P.M. on a surprisingly warm evening in early October. Jerry Falwell has just climbed into his Suburban Wagon and is headed home from the Lynchburg Municipal Airport. He has had a typically busy day and has left the bedraggled co-workers who accompanied him on his day's activities with a word that he is tired and will spend a quiet evening at home—a rare luxury for him.

Jerry's day began at dawn when he rose to spend a quiet hour in prayer and Bible study. He arrived at the Lynchburg airport only minutes before a 6:45 A.M. flight to New York. In Manhattan he spoke on a live television talk show, answering rapid-fire questions telephoned in from the show's viewing audience.

Today Jerry was accompanied by two of his staff members, with whom he discussed business affairs during travel time, and by the student body president of Liberty Baptist College, who, aspiring to be a pastor, was being given the chance to be near Jerry and learn from him. The group traveled from New York to the U.S. Senate Office Building in Washington, D.C., where they dined with

Senator Jesse Helms and spent time with him in his Senate office.

Now twelve-year-old Jonathan is waiting at the window for his dad. As soon as he sees the familiar blue wagon round the corner and come up the drive, he is out of the house at breakneck speed. "Dad! Dad!" he yells before Jerry has had time to stop, "They just called and said they have front row seats for us at the Yankees' game in New York. They said they'd fly us up and everything and have a taxi waiting at the airport to take us right to the game! Jerry Jr. can't go, but will you take me?"

In less than five minutes Jerry is headed for the shower. "Macel, honey," he calls, "will you fix me a peanut butter sandwich?" Thirty minutes after pulling in the drive, Jerry and exuberant Jonathan are headed for the Lynchburg Municipal Airport. Jerry has found the needed energy somewhere.

Everyone who knows Jerry Falwell knows that Jesus Christ is first in his life and that next in priority is his family—his wife Macel and their three children, Jerry Jr., Jeannie, and Jonathan. He likes the loose paraphrase of Mark 8:36, which states, "For what shall it profit a man if he gains the whole world but loses his own children?"

"Apart from our devotion to Christ," says Jerry, "Macel and I love and live for our children. We really don't have anything in this world that one day won't be theirs. Everything we talk about and plan around is for their benefit and welfare. The longer we live, the more we want to invest in them. They mean everything to us. Our first obligation is to rear godly children, for it is God who gave them to us. The greatest desire of our hearts for our children is that they each find God's will and live in it all their days."

Macel and Jerry share a warm and mutually rewarding relationship. Jerry includes his wife in many of his activities, and from Macel, Jerry receives an abundant share of love and concern and the encouragement needed to tackle his tremendous responsibilities. Macel, who was at Jerry's side the day Thomas Road Baptist Church was organized, has played a vital role in the development of the ministry. But foremost she has been a good wife and mother.

Many times Jerry is asked by magazine interviewers if he plans special activities with his children and if there is some "formula" he would like to pass along to their readers. His replies vary but include the following points: "Jesus Christ is first in our family. Ours is a happy home because of that priority. We believe in togetherness and spend much time together. As a preacher of the gospel, I am extremely busy. But I try not to fool myself; I should never be too busy to spend time with my family and with each child individually. My wife's phone calls are always put through to me, regardless of what I am doing."

Jerry's vast ministry to people necessitates that he travel a greal deal. When he is away from home, he calls Macel and his children at least once a day. He talks to Macel, Jerry Jr., Jeannie, and Jonathan and prays with each individually. He often says to mothers and fathers, "You had better make your family your priority, because that is God's priority for you. You may have all the world against you, but if you have a loving spouse and children who love one another, your home will be a fortress. It will be a refuge to which you run. A true Christian home is the most heavenly thing on this earth. It is characterized by peace and serenity and is a place of happiness."

Jerry goes to great lengths to spend time with his children. Before Jerry Jr. received his driver's license, Jerry would drive the children to school regardless of what time he had arrived home the previous night. Jerry talks much about his children. "Jerry Jr. is taller than I am now. He's sixteen and a junior in high school. I don't like to say that, because it reminds me that next year he will be a senior; he will go to college and soon be gone.

"Little Jeannie is fourteen. I know she's not perfect, but I don't know anything about her that isn't—my wife could tell you a few things! She's still Grampa's little girl and a real doll.

"Jonathan is our twelve-year-old, red-headed stick of dynamite. The other day I was having a high-level meeting with bankers, discussing millions of dollars. Jonathan came bouncing in selling some candy for a class project. He made several sales in the office that day."

In recent years Jerry has adopted the practice of taking a one-month summer vacation with his family. The Falwells strike out in a motor home on an unscheduled trip in the United States and Canada. Sometimes there are slight problems along the way. Jerry's recognition factor is such that he must avoid large resorts and busy recreational areas. Several years ago the Falwell family visited Disneyland, but it took them several hours just to get past the front gate. Jerry was mobbed by autograph hunters and people who wanted to talk with him. Sometimes even the sanctity of a vacation must be interrupted by an emergency or the press of business, and Jerry is forced to fly back to Lynchburg. At those times Jerry Jr. takes the wheel of the camper.

When he was only twelve years old, Jerry Jr. proved his resourcefulness by helping his mother prepare for an unexpected trip to Egypt. His Dad was already in Cairo, when he called and asked Macel and the children to join him there. Jerry Jr. made all the arrangements and even did much of the packing. When he was younger, Jerry Jr. often used to travel with his dad, but now he would rather go up to a mountaintop cabin where he can have his dad all to himself.

As great as the pressures of notoriety are for Jerry Falwell, they are also felt by his immediate family. Macel has learned to deal with this constant phenomenon; she takes being Jerry's wife very much in stride. To Macel, Jerry has never changed. "He's never gotten too big for his position," she says. "He treats people the same today as when we had thirty-five members at Thomas Road. He's basically the same person I've always known."

From Jerry, Macel has learned to believe God for great things. "I remember the first time Jerry came home and told me he was going to add on to our building," she reminisces. "I thought, *Really, you shouldn't do it, because you're not going to fill it up, and it's going to look bad. The place will be half empty.* And then, of course, it was packed from the first day. And I remember the time Jerry said he was going to buy Treasure Island. I said, 'Jerry, you can't do that. Where will the money come from? How are you going to use it?' And of course, it has proven to be a great ministry. I have finally learned to take whatever Jerry says and accept it because what he says always happens, and that is because the Lord directs him. I truly believe that Jerry lives so close to the Lord that he gets the desires of his heart."

"How strong is a man?" Jerry Falwell asks his congregation and the approximately twenty million viewers of the *Old-Time Gospel Hour*. "He is only as strong as is his relationship to Christ. When a father is rightly related to the Lord and has unbroken fellowship with God, he has all the strength and authority of the living Christ vested in him. When this kind of a dad leads his family, they will

believe in him and love and respect him. It will be an honor
for children to follow in his footsteps.''

Jerry Jr., Jeannie, and Jonathan love their father deeply
and are proud to follow in his footsteps. They obey him
out of love and have learned that love necessitates discipline.

One Sunday morning when Macel had her leg in a cast
and could not drive, arrangements had to be made for
them to get to church, since each had to be there at
different times.

Jonathan came down the stairs from his bedroom and
said, ''Well, mommy can't drive. Are we still going?''

Jerry replied, ''Oh, yes, you know you are.''

''Do we get a vote?'' Jonathan asked.

''You never have gotten a vote have you?'' Jerry replied.

''Nope,'' said Jonathan laughing, ''only one vote here,
and that one is yours, Dad.''

It is a sad fact that there are today few solid families and
homes in our nation where love and unity between parents
and children reign. That is why a central theme of many of
Jerry Falwell's sermons is the home and family. ''I am for
the family,'' says Jerry. ''I am committed to helping
families win the undeclared war that is ravaging American
homes. Each family is a battleground for the conflict going
on today. The consequences of defeat are tragic.'' Evidence in America today shows that many battles are being
lost.

''The Christian family is the basic unit in society so far
as God is concerned,'' Jerry preaches. ''No nation has
ever been any stronger than the families within her. When
the family begins to falter, when that basic Christian unit is

slowly destroyed as is happening in our country today, we are on the precipice of real peril.

"Hollywood has declared war on the monogamous Christian home. The major networks are all allowing major prime-time programs that honor divorce, glorify broken homes, and give creditability to homosexuals. According to a recent Gallup Poll, problems such as use of drugs, vandalism, and parental lack of interest face American public schools. Public schools have many problems, but number one is lack of discipline. It all begins in the home.

"If America is going to stand, she must get back to the Word of God and back to holy living in her homes. There is no way to enjoy success apart from God's blueprint. It makes no difference that our society is quite sophisticated and very educated. Men cannot do what is right in their own eyes, disregard God's immutable laws, and expect to be blessed of God. Americans have cheapened the institution that is most precious to God upon this earth, the home, and we are seeing the consequences in America's stability as a nation. Parents dare not think that they can turn their backs on their God-given responsibilities and get away with it. Someday, children will either rise up and call their parents blessed, or they will curse their memory.

"We have in our nation today weak men trying to head up families. Men who are not rightly related to the Lord Jesus Christ are unable to give the spiritual leadership needed to their wives and children. No wonder we are raising up a generation of children who have no respect for authority, civil or otherwise. They have been reared in homes where there is no authority and in which there is no guidance or leadership. Children need love, discipline, and parental example. When children grow up without ever learning what the Bible has to say, without ever learning what prayer is, and without ever having been brought into and trained by a good, Bible-believing, soul-winning local church, they become weak people who in turn reproduce weak homes.

"What is the answer? The answer is not just to curse the darkness. The answer is to light a few candles. I would like to say to every dad in America: If you love this nation and you want your children to have the kind of America you have enjoyed, establish a Christian home. It is your responsibility to do it. Do not pass that on to your wife, Dad; this is your responsibility. As a dad under God you are to establish a home in which there is Bible reading, prayer, church attendance, holy living, and clean language and behavior. To every mother I would like to say: You have greater influence upon your children than any other human being on this earth. See to it that your children have a godly mother, that your habits are clean, your language pure, and your example good. Lead your children in submission to their dad and to you. Lead them to the house of God along with you and your husband. See that they get at home the spiritual influence they ought to have.

"Children are a heritage of the Lord. God has promised that if parents will train up their children in the way they should go, when their children are old, they will not depart from it. How then can a dad and mom deal with the fact that their children are in a society filled with permissiveness and in atmospheres of immorality, in a world of music that is perverted, and in a world of many dress styles that are immoral? How can a dad and mom today insist that their sons and daughters be different? They can do this only as they stand fast in the Lord and set a godly example before those sons and daughters."

Chapter 13

By All Means

. . . I am made all things to all men, that I might by all means
save some (1 Cor. 9:22).

It is 10:59 on a Sunday morning, and the congregation of
the Thomas Road Baptist Church is relaxed, waiting for
the beginning of the morning service. High above the
sanctuary, however, in a glass enclosed booth, an air of
tension prevails. Eleven pairs of eyes are fixed on television monitors, while in the chair closest to the window, a
curly-haired young man listens intently to a countdown:
60 . . . 59 . . . 58 . . .

"There are problems, guys," says the director. "Camera
number one can't hear me, and camera number four is
tearing up the picture. Before the panic sets in, let's
pray." He bows his head and prays quickly, "Our
heavenly Father, we thank You for the medium of television. We pray for the technical aspects of this program so
we can produce a show worthy of Your Son, Jesus
Christ." He looks up . . . 24 . . . 23 . . . 22 . . . "Camera
number two ready to pan. . . ." A crew of professionally
trained technicians moves into action.

Bruce Braun, who once worked for the ABC television
network on the West Coast, directs the taping of the
Old-Time Gospel Hour, which in four weeks will be aired
by 327 stations to an audience numbering twenty million
people. He has been working since 6:00 A.M., preparing

119

for the taping. He has gone over the program schedule with Don Norman, the show's executive producer, and with Jerry. "I have never been associated with anyone as easy to work with as Jerry," says Bruce. "He is quick and has a keen understanding of technique."

As the service proceeds, two production assistants hang on Bruce's every word, carefully logging and time-coding each shot. Altogether about seventy minutes of tape will roll through the control room's machines, and on Monday morning Bruce will begin the laborious task of editing down the material to a final program of fifty-eight minutes, thirty seconds. When the editing is completed, the tape will be air-freighted to the headquarters of National Educational Television (NET) in Ann Arbor, Michigan, where through the use of high speed equipment duplicate copies—at the rate of six every six minutes—will be fabricated. NET's syndication service will then send the tapes to the stations forming the Old-Time Gospel Hour network, which is today the largest independent network in the United States.

When asked his ultimate dream, Jerry Falwell says, "I believe this is the terminal generation before Jesus comes. My ultimate desire is to glorify God by giving the gospel of Jesus Christ to every creature in my generation—somehow." It is that "somehow" that has convinced him that the mediums of television, radio, and the printed page can be greatly used to efficiently spread the gospel. Jerry says, "There are 4.4 billion people in our world today. Jesus Christ died for every one of them. The return of the Lord is imminent. We have a very short time in which to do a mammoth task. It is our conviction that God gave us the mass media to get the gospel out to as many as possible in these last days."

Jerry had long been interested in radio. He had first heard the gospel through Charles E. Fuller's *Old-Fashioned Revival Hour* and began the *Old-Time Gospel Hour* radio broadcast soon after the Thomas Road Church was organized in 1956. A daily one-half hour of broadcast time was purchased, and for a number of years Jerry drove to the radio station and made the broadcasts live each morning at 6:30. After a few years equipment was purchased, and the broadcast went out live from Jerry's study each morning at 9:00.

Today more than four hundred radio stations carry the *Old-Time Gospel Hour* across the nation. A conversational Bible study approach has resulted in effective communication of the gospel. Thousands of letters come in to the Jerry Falwell Ministries yearly from people whose lives have been influenced by the program.

"I was driving home from a large business convention," wrote one businessman, "when I tuned in to your radio program. It was a good thing I did. I did not want to go home. I was depressed. At the convention I had spent time drinking and carousing. After listening to Jerry Falwell's message for a few minutes, God broke my heart. I pulled my car over to the side of the road and there accepted Jesus Christ as my personal Savior. I have found purpose in life. My home is a different place."

The Thomas Road television ministry was begun six months after the church was founded. For the first eleven years, the program was broadcast from a studio; then in 1968 it was decided to televise the Sunday morning worship service. In 1970, the church made a considerable investment in color equipment, and the next year the program moved from a regional to a national basis.

The *Old-Time Gospel Hour* television program thrives on its sincerity and identity. People who tune in like to feel they are at a Sunday morning church service. They can relate to the pastor, the music, the program's regulars, the crying baby, the fellow yawning in the choir, and the late-comers walking in the aisles. They see a church service with cameras looking on instead of a television production with an audience looking on. "People who are hurting don't want to see a show," says Jerry, "They want to see something that is real."

Over the years, hundreds of experts have written, called, or personally told Jerry how to improve the show. They have suggested changes, like putting potted plants on the platform, having special audience inserts, or applying other techniques; Jerry, however, has steadfastly resisted all these attempts to change the program's basic formula.

"These professionals just don't have the slightest idea of what makes our show tick," he says. The program's director, Bruce Braun—who believes the primary purpose of the broadcast is to communicate the spirit and atmosphere of a church service—admits, "Some of the things we do are against all the television textbooks."

Jerry's goal is to bring the entire *Old-Time Gospel Hour* into prime time. He does not, however, believe that a television service should replace church attendance and membership and encourages those who write him to become involved in a local church. "Television can never replace the local church. In fact, unless we are complementing the local church, we are failing our mission. I am a television preacher, not a television pastor. There can never be a substitute for the local church."

One night Jerry spoke in a coliseum in Ohio. A gentleman came up to him, shook his hand, and said, "You don't know me, but three years ago you helped change my life. I was two minutes from hell. I had been an alcoholic for eleven years and was about to end it all when I heard you say, on TV, 'God loves you.' I felt those words were directed to me. I woke my family . . . we started going to church. We are all born again. We are new people.'' The man had no idea why the *Old-Time Gospel Hour* was on that night. He had no explanation for why he even heard what Jerry was saying, but God had had it all planned.

After Jerry preached in a church in Pennsylvania recently, an elderly lady insisted on talking to him personally. She told Jerry a story about her husband who, though seventy years old, had never attended a church service in his life. At one time in his life he had claimed to be an atheist, but two years earlier he had begun to watch the *Old-Time Gospel Hour.* His wife had seen a difference in him almost every week since he had started watching the program. Finally, just two weeks earlier, while watching the *Old-Time Gospel Hour,* he had received Jesus Christ as his Lord and Savior. Two days later this man had died suddenly of a heart attack. The lady hugged Jerry and thanked him profusely. ''If it had not been for the *Old-Time Gospel Hour,''* she cried, ''my husband would be dead and in hell. I would have had no hope of ever seeing him again.''

More than thirty thousand letters reporting a spiritual decision flood the offices of the Jerry Falwell Ministries yearly. Many of them come from people requesting follow-up material because they have made a decision for Jesus Christ. Other letters come from those who are bedridden or who are physically unable to go to church. Thousands write to relate varied stories of blessings. A grandmother wrote,

> Your program and the records from your ministry mean much to my daughter who has a retarded daughter, age seven. Your records are played to her during every waking

hour she lives. She responds only to that music. It is so
soothing to her. It is an inspiration to us. We thank you for
your God-anointed ministry.

A young man wrote,

Through watching the *Old-Time Gospel Hour* program I
realized my need of a Savior. Now I watch you every
Sunday before I leave for Sunday school. I thank God
every day for what he has done for me and for your ministry. I just can't tell you how good it is to know God and to
walk with Him.

A mother and father wrote,

Being parents of a severely handicapped young child (as
well as three healthy children) has made one or the other of
us 'shut-ins' for nearly six years now. Your television
programs and various outreach programs have brought to
us many things we could never otherwise hear or participate in. I can't tell you how many times the music, the
testimonies, and the sermons have changed our 'downs' to
'ups' and given us the strength to face a new week. The
Lord has provided more than ample strength and love to us
all in our family. Your ministries have enhanced our lives
so much. We thank you!

Four million people in America and Canada are wearing
pins that say, "Jesus First." These are given to anyone
who asks for them. They are a public testimony to the
preeminence of Jesus Christ in the lives of individuals. A
young lady wrote,

I was born again in November, 1977, because of your
ministry. Through the *Old-Time Gospel Hour* I heard the
true meaning and full understanding of John 3:16. The Holy

Spirit has filled me with the love of Jesus Christ. About a month ago I was home sick on Sunday. I turned on the television and there you were, Dr. Falwell. Your message touched me to the point of rededication of my life to the Lord. My first prayer was to be a better witness for my Lord. The answer came not five minutes later when you said anyone could write for a "Jesus First" pin. I am a waitress, and my husband is a corpsman in the Navy. We both come in contact with many people. You pin is a small object, but its meaning is great. Please send us two pins so by wearing them doors might be opened for us to help other people. Thank you. We love you.

Only eternity will reveal how far-reaching are the results of the various daily ministries of the Thomas Road Baptist Church. Sometimes God permits those who have been deeply blessed to share their testimony with the congregation.

On a Wednesday evening in March, 1979, two brothers who pastor a church in the South visited Thomas Road and shared what the Jerry Falwell Ministries and the *Old-Time Gospel Hour* had meant and still means to them. David began: "My brother and I have not always been Baptists. We went to our former denomination's seminary and attended all their seminars. They told us that every night after you preach you ought to go home and watch a little television to unwind. One night I unwound on the *Old-Time Gospel Hour*. Dr. Falwell preached, and I got excited! I'd never seen anything like what I saw on the *Old-Time Gospel Hour* that evening. I called my brother Steve and told him to turn on the television. I said, 'Steve, there are people everywhere in that church! They're singing and preaching. People are getting saved.'

"Steve and I began to watch the program regularly, and God spoke to our hearts. We began to preach to our congregation the way Dr. Falwell preached. We began to stand up for the Lord. We caught Dr. Falwell's vision and determined to build a great church and do something for God. A few points of doctrine Dr. Falwell preached did not agree with ours. We searched the Word of God and changed our minds about certain things. We went out and bought five buses. Our attendance doubled.

"About that time we began to get into trouble. The stewards called us in. They said, 'We want to tell you two that these dirty little kids don't belong in our church. For the first time in the history of this church, we've got bubble gum under our pews. We had to get some special remover because there was a big lump on our beautiful red carpet where one of them dropped a sucker. These kids have got to go. The buses cost too much to run. Besides, they weren't in the budget.' We told them they were not going to go, that we were going to run the buses and preach the Word of God.

"One morning Steve and I were working at the church when the county sheriff delivered us a summons. We were to appear at the county courthouse two weeks from that day. Big headlines across the papers read, 'Church Sues Pastors.' We went through some very dark days. I asked Steve how we had ever gotten ourselves into such a mess. We were just trying to win souls. What happened?

"Two weeks passed, and we found ourselves in the courtroom, sitting before a judge like two criminals. The judge asked, 'What have these fellows done?' The stewards had rounded up fourteen witnesses. One lady testified, 'Judge, they're never satisfied. They want the whole city in our church, no matter who they are.' Another lady said, 'They preach too long. The kids they bus in are dirty.' Then another witness said, 'They have been listening to some fellow on television and they've quit reading certain of our creeds and quoting some of our canons.''

''The judge told us to either get out of the church or do what the stewards said. We didn't know what to do. Every week for twelve weeks some of our strong supporters gathered with us, and we watched the *Old-Time Gospel Hour* together. We listened carefully to very word Dr. Falwell preached.

''I wanted to quit . . . It was a difficult time, but I kept listening to Dr. Falwell's preaching: 'Stand in the gap. Be God's man. Do what you know God wants you to do.' Finally I told Steve that I would resign and that he should stay with the people until we could decide what to do. The *Old-Time Gospel Hour* broadcast kept us going. We were fed by it every Sunday night and would go out into battle all week long.

''We didn't want to let that church go. We had worked hard there. We had five buses, $12,000 worth of printing equipment, and a $200,000 building. Most of it had been built up while we were there. Then one Sunday night Dr. Falwell said, 'Everything you give up for God, God will give back to you a hundred fold.' Steve and I prayed, 'God, we will give it all.' We got a little white house and started a church. It was the ugliest house you have ever seen. It's amazing that people even came there to worship. Our names had been in the headlines; no businesses in town trusted us. About that time Dr. Falwell announced the Super Conference at Thomas Road Baptist Church. I was very down and discouraged but told Steve I had to go.

''When I arrived at Thomas Road I looked at your great work, at the grounds, the mountain, your excited people, and the exuberant young people in the schools. I thought of the thirty-five people who had stuck with us through our mess and thought of how Dr. Falwell had started Thomas

Road with only thirty-five people. As I walked on the grounds I prayed, 'Oh, God, use us somehow.' That night Dr. Falwell preached a sermon entitled 'The God of All Encouragement.' I sat and literally wept. God began to feed my soul, and I cried out to Him, 'God, can it be so? Can you use me? Can Steve and I do that?' Back in my motel room I cried all night.

"The next morning I was the first one in the church. I wanted the front row seat. Dr. Falwell preached, 'Be a Champion.' I drank in every vibration. My heart cheered up, and I began to feel like shouting. My heart cried out, 'We can do it. God, here am I; use me; use Steve. Let us stand in the gap for You. Let Steve and I build a church for You.' I knew something was going to happen. I soaked up everything in that conference and couldn't wait to get home. I called Steve and said, 'Steve, we're on the move!'

"Soon Steve and I bought a bus. We got on the radio. We started a Christian school in a garage with seven children. We began to systematically take our town for the Lord. Every day we'd go out and knock on doors. We had heard Dr. Falwell say, 'Knock on every door in your city.' We began to lead people to Jesus. We were alive. God was blessing us. Everything Dr. Falwell would say on the *Old-Time Gospel Hour,* we would turn around and do it. We had problems, but we weren't afraid of giants anymore. We worked hard all week, preached hard on Sunday, and then on Sunday nights our people would go home and the whole church would watch the *Old-Time Gospel Hour.* Your singing groups came and ministered to us, and some of your great men came and preached for us.

"It is four years now since we started our church. We have known what it means to pay a price. We grew much in that little white house. We rented the house next door and filled it up. We got up to 163 people in those two houses and the garage. Then we leased the YWCA. The second year we went up to 345. We just had to buy land, but we didn't have any money. Our people sacrificed greatly. We bought five acres. So many miracles happened. About the time your ministry desperately needed $7 million, we needed $25,000. Dr. Falwell told about the time God brought him to the place where he had to relinquish control of his ministry and offer it to God and just be a steward. Dr. Falwell said, 'We must have this money if we are to go on. It is in God's hands. It is His ministry, and He can do with it what He wants to.' So we said the same thing. If Dr. Falwell could believe God for $7 million, we could believe God for $25,000.

"God supplied it miraculously! We expanded our school and built another building. Two weeks ago we had more than fourteen hundred people packed into that building. We have a fleet of twelve buses. There are more than two hundred children in our school. We have twenty-two acres of land that is valued at a half million dollars.

"We love you Thomas Roaders. We feel like we belong to your church. You stand in the gap for America. Dr. Falwell often stands alone. Never get discouraged. There are others like us who need your example desperately and who are looking to you today."

Chapter 14

A Man Of Action

I must work the works of him that sent me, while it is day: the night cometh, when no man can work (John 9:4).

A large crowd stands milling about the platform in the Murfreesboro (Tennessee) Convention Hall. It is 11:00 P.M. on a hot, sticky June evening. For more than three hours, the folks now gathered at the front of the auditorium have listened to two of the major personalities of twentieth-century American fundamentalism. One, the elder statesman of the movement, John R. Rice, has been toiling in the fundamentalist vineyard for well over sixty years. The other man, a relative newcomer compared to Rice's tenure, has in the last decade overshadowed his contemporaries and become the driving force behind the movement's renaissance.

As Jerry Falwell smiles, chats, and fixes his autograph inside several Bibles, he must be tired. This has been a long and exhausting day—like most for a very busy man.

It started early at 6:00 A.M. After five hours of sleep, Jerry arose, showered, and read from his well-worn Bible. After breakfast and a time of devotions with his family, Jerry climbed into his suburban wagon and drove off to an early morning staff meeting at the church. When he arrived at his office, Jeannette Hogan, his personal secretary of eighteen years, handed him a lengthy list of telephone calls that had already come in. She also gave Jerry a sheaf of correspondence, including some of the approximately two hundred letters that he personally answers each week. Jeannette had also prepared a tentative schedule for the day and a list of those individuals who most urgently require Jerry's time.

Once he had settled in at his large desk, Jerry dialed the interoffice telephone and spoke to Nelson Keener, his young and efficient administrative assistant. Nelson fed him information about the Murfreesboro trip, including church departure and flight times, as well as the names of the key people involved in the evening's program. Nelson, among other major responsibilities, is charged with developing Jerry's out-of-town schedule. In addition to tonight's Sword of the Lord Conference, Nelson has booked Jerry for the next few weeks to speak at several churches, Christian schools, coliseums, stewardship dinners, a television talk show, and a rally. This is in addition to special meetings, funerals, and weddings at Thomas Road Baptist Church.

At 10:00 A.M., Jerry attended a meeting of his top staff. Although he listened carefully and intently to each man's report, the burden of responsibility for the overall program was clearly upon his shoulders.

By noon he was ready for lunch. He has a few favorite places in town, and almost invariably his meals are interrupted by friends or other people who recognize him. Jerry takes advantage of his lunch hour to talk to staff members of the church or to administrators of the Liberty Baptist Schools. Many days Jerry dines with preachers, teachers, or media people who come to Lynchburg to view the Jerry Falwell Ministries or to seek counsel.

The early part of this particular afternoon was taken up by personal interviews. All types of people with all kinds of purposes in mind wanted to see Jerry. At 3:30 P.M.,

Jerry, who sometimes runs late, was already twenty minutes behind takeoff time. Nelson finally got him out of the office and drove him to the Lynchburg Municipal Airport where a chartered jet awaited Jerry and the small entourage that joined him for the Murfreesboro trip.

Just before the jet took off, one of the men prayed for safety on their journey. The people who accompany Jerry on his trips are not chosen at random. Jerry conducts a considerable amount of business during the many hours each year he spends in the air.

When the plane touched down in Nashville, the jet taxied to the private craft sector of the field. Lynchburg's relative inaccessibility makes it impossible for Jerry to regularly fly on commercial airplanes. Without these chartered flights he could not fulfill his incredibly busy and complex schedule.

Jerry is always able to relax and unwind aboard an airplane. Air travel is so much a part of his life that he often employs this subject in sermon illustrations. "You know, when I hear of pessimism, I think of what it's like to get in an airplane on a rainy day. You put yourself in the pilot's hands, and then you sit back and in a little while you're up above the clouds. The sun is shining, and your whole outlook on the day has changed. That's the way life is. Even when you can't see the sun, you've got to realize it's shining. So get above the clouds, work your way up and around the negative people, the pessimists, the critics, and the cynics."

There was no limousine waiting to whisk Jerry to his speaking engagement. Instead, a fairly battered van with rather inadequate air conditioning carried him to the Nashville suburbs. When the van pulled up to the Sheraton hotel it was several minutes past six o'clock. There was only enough time for Jerry to check in and change his shirt. At seven he had to be in his place on the platform, listening to John Rice preach.

Jerry had prepared his message well. It was directed to Christians, since most of those in attendance were full-time church workers. He spoke to them on the theme of "building a wall," using the experiences of the biblical Nehemiah as his focal point. Before he entered the main body of his message, he shared some heart-to-heart sentiments. "We need to plant more good, Bible-believing churches in every city in America. We need to plant thousands of them. We need to send out thousands of missionaries. We need to raise up workers. We need to be winning souls constantly and increasing the ranks, increasing the numbers of the fundamentalists.

"It is my conviction that in the next twenty years, if the Lord has not returned, America could experience what I call a real local church revival that could change the course of this nation's future. If we get enough preachers, enough churches, enough Bible teachers, and enough saints, numerically one day we can make the difference."

When the service ended, Jerry waited to personally greet anyone who wished to meet and talk to him, even though he had a major business session scheduled for late in the evening. Many people came up to shake Jerry's hand and share a word with him. There was the teenaged girl who told him she was preparing to come to Liberty Baptist College in the fall, the elderly but spritely woman who informed Jerry she is a Faith Partner (one who supports the Thomas Road ministries), the boat captain who told Jerry he bought a television set just to watch the *Old-Time Gospel Hour* on his runs up and down the East Coast. A freckled-faced, eleven-year-old lad shyly said to Jerry, "I really enjoyed your message"; the city manager of Murfreesboro assured Jerry that he watches him every

Sunday. A Reverend Johnson, a young black pastor from Atlanta, exclaimed, "You look just like you do on TV!" And a middle-aged farmer thanked Jerry for the Liberty Home Bible Institute, which, he added, had been "a great blessing."

As the long line thinned, a young woman in a wheel chair was put in front of Jerry. She had spent the last eighteen months paralyzed from the waist down as the result of an automobile accident. The young woman smiled radiantly. Jerry knelt down and spent several minutes talking with her.

At 11:30 P.M., Jerry was running well behind schedule. At the Sheraton a group of people were awaiting his arrival. One of these individuals, a celebrated British film producer, came to Tennessee to show Jerry several films based on biblical events and personalities. At 12:30 A.M., after being stopped in the hotel lobby by several people, Jerry finally came into the meeting. A half hour later someone realized that everyone's last meal had been at lunchtime and one of the group was dispatched to an all-night, fast-food restaurant. At 2:30 A.M. Jerry broke up the meeting. His next appointment was a 7:00 A.M. breakfast.

While no two days in Jerry's life are alike, this twenty-four-hour period could be described as normal. It was typical in the sense that his time was taken up with meetings, decisions, personal encounters, public addresses, and a host of other activities. Many marvel at Jerry's pace. Yet he is never too busy to surprise the students at the Liberty Baptist Schools by stopping by their classes and activities. Every weekend Jerry can be seen in the hospitals in Lynchburg. He says he has learned the secret of praying without ceasing, "As I hurry about the day's activities, I am constantly talking to God."

Inquisitive reporters around the country scurry to keep up with Jerry when he appears in their city. Jerry has been featured in many of the major magazines and newspapers in America. "There are the Bible-thumping, 'Thank you, Jesus,' blues-shouting evangelists. And then there is Jerry Falwell," said an article in the *Houston Post*.

"Evangelist Helps Raise a Hope, a Prayer and Money for Prop. 6. By the thousands they came last night—in buses and cars and pickup trucks and campers—" reported the *San Diego Union*.

"If America gets by with her sin, God will owe an apology to Sodom and Gomorrah . . ." the *Detroit Free Press* quoted Jerry. The *Wall Street Journal* described him as "a man of charm, talent, drive, and ambition."

Normally Jerry speaks publicly twenty times a week. He often jokes, "When I die, my vocal cords will say 'thanks.' " He considers it a great privilege and makes it a priority to speak at the anniversary celebrations of those young men who have gone out from the Liberty Baptist Schools to start their own churches. Almost seven hundred people attended the first anniversary service of Lamarr Mooneyham's church. Lamarr recalls what Jerry always told the preacher boys at LBC: "Before you go to a town to start a church, go alone to the city limits. Place your hand on the city limits sign and ask God to give you every person in that city. Claim that city for Jesus Christ, and learn to pray and weep over it. John Knox was able to win Scotland, because on the shores of that nation he prayed, 'O God, give me Scotland or I die.' "

Before Jerry comes to preach, Cliff Hartley tells his people, "Jeannie and I will never be able to express what

Thomas Road Baptist Church, Liberty Baptist College, and Dr. Jerry Falwell have meant to our lives and to this ministry. At Liberty Baptist College our lives were transformed. I left there with a three-point outline for my ministry. Jerry always said first, 'Nothing of eternal value is ever accomplished apart from prayer;' second, 'The difference between greatness and mediocrity is vision;' and third, 'You determine a man's greatness not by his talent or wealth as the world does, but rather by what it takes to discourage him.' "

Al Henson, pastor of Light House Baptist Church in Nashville, earned a degree in engineering from the University of Tennessee and later worked for the Federal Land Bank. He gave up a promising career in federal service to study at LBC.

After his training he went to Nashville and began to knock on doors. A few days later he and his wife met with three people in their apartment. Two weeks later forty-two people attended their first worship service in the recreation room of their apartment complex. After five months, the church purchased twenty-five acres of land near a large shopping center and began meeting in a farmhouse on the property. Nine months after Henson began his initial round of visitation, about 175 people were coming to Sunday services. The church's first anniversary was celebrated by more than 900 people in an outdoor service.

"A hundred percent of what I know, I've learned from Jerry Falwell," says Henson. "You don't copy what he does, but you apply his methods within your own context."

A letter was received at the Jerry Falwell Ministries from a man in Pennsylvania.

We pledged one hundred dollars to help a student last year . . . We send our contribution on a monthly basis and still have one month to go on that pledge. We would like to join again for another one hundred dollars for a student for the coming semester. You mentioned that students from Liberty Baptist College go out after graduation to set this world on fire for Jesus. You are not kidding. One is doing just that. You should see the glow and vision and compassion of this godly man, John Cartwright. He and his family are here in Sharon Hill, Pennsylvania, where the Lord is doing great things.

It would surprise most of the people who ask "How in the world does Jerry Falwell keep up with such a busy schedule?" to know that Jerry does not enjoy constant travel. One thing keeps him going; he has one goal, one purpose, one obsession—to win men and women to Jesus Christ. "Anything worthwhile, anything that has the sanction of God, costs a great price," Jerry tells young preachers. "Redemption came at a great price. Building a super-aggressive local church comes at a great price. Salvation is free, but delivering the message of salvation costs. It costs to build and propagate and deliver the message of the gospel. Blood, sweat, tears, heartaches, and heartbreaks have gone behind this work. But when you see lives and families transformed, you know you could never do anything else. You can mark it down—if there is a message going out that is powerful, someone has paid a price somewhere." Part of the price for Jerry includes traveling more than two hundred thousand miles annually.

Jerry Falwell believes in hard work. He averaged a hundred house calls a day the first few years he pastored Thomas Road Baptist Church, because he sees people as either going to heaven or to hell, depending on what they have done about Jesus Christ. "We are living in a discouraged, despairing world," he says from his pulpit. "Lately God has been waking me up at night. I have been getting up early and going down late, and in airplanes and in all kinds of places, I have found myself asking God for revival and asking God to make me fit for the task. I want to be a vessel unto honor, meet for the Master's use. I have been asking God to give me messages that convey what He is trying to say. I want God to speak through me. We must all be receptive to the voice of the Holy Spirit in these last days."

Jerry's anticipation of the Second Coming of Jesus Christ stiffens his resolve to bring the gospel to every person. The long days, the endless round of meetings and travel, the sermons, messages, and speeches that form the work cycle of his life are intimately related to this expectation.

Jerry says, "The coming of Jesus Christ could occur any moment. Christians look forward to His coming. When Christ returns, every believer of the New Testament era will be raptured away. Our entire social order will then be set in disarray. While millions of believers will instantly be caught up to be with the Lord and will disappear from the human scene, the remainder of the earth's population will be left behind for the beginning of the Tribulation Period. The headlines of major newspapers will read, 'Multitudes Missing.' "

Jerry talks in earnest to the members of the Thomas Road Baptist Church. "In the brief time before us before the coming of Jesus Christ, we have the responsibility of propagating the gospel of our Lord and Savior to more than four billion souls. If we are going to be successful in preaching the gospel to every creature, then we cannot have any cop-outs or casualties in the ranks. Every one of us must be on top spiritually. The apostle Paul said, 'Let us not be weary in well doing: for in due season we shall reap, if we faint not.' God's mercies are new every morning. He causes us to triumph in Christ.

"Many of you today are discouraged and defeated. You are contemplating quitting. I have been in the work of the Lord for twenty-seven years and have been the pastor of this church for twenty-three years. I can recount to you some pressures and problems that I have faced that in all honesty I wondered if it would not be better to quit. I thank God that I didn't.

"Men ought always to pray and not to faint. There have been times when I stood up in this pulpit physically down, feeling very bad. Feeling sick, I have looked out at thousands of people and thought of the millions behind the television cameras and prayed, 'Lord, I'm not able to do it today. I just don't know how in the world I'm going to do it today. You must do for me what I cannot do for myself.' Then God has put in my head and in my heart just the words He wanted me to speak; one sentence after another fell into place. And somewhere out there, suddenly all the weariness had gone and the freshness of thought and the freedom of expression had supernaturally come from God, and I was able to deliver God's message. That is true in every area of life. No matter what you do; wait on the Lord, and He will renew your strength."

There are thousands of people around this world who are very thankful that Jerry Falwell has found the secret of waiting on God for renewed strength. Although he preaches to multitudes each week, he does not see a sea of faces when he preaches; he sees individuals and realizes there are many broken and hurting people in each crowd he preaches to. This is why he spends many hours talking to individuals and listening attentively to everything they have to say. When Jerry returns to a city after a year's absence he recalls by name the majority of those people he met the year before. Although God has seen fit to send the Thomas Road Baptist Church and the Liberty Baptist College some large financial gifts, it is the widow who hands Jerry an envelope with a sacrificial gift of $10 in it that makes his eyes mist.

Two brothers who attended Liberty Baptist Seminary and now pastor a church in Oregon remember Jerry's influence on their lives. "I went to Lynchburg to attend Liberty Baptist Seminary in August, 1975," said Bob Gass. "I went because I wanted to be a soul-winning pastor and do a great work for God . . . The most important thing I learned from Dr. Falwell concerning the ministry was that a pastor must love his people. I learned much from Dr. Falwell's preaching and teaching, but this I didn't have to be told; I could plainly see it in his life . . . I have seen him stand by while others made unjust, unkind accusations about him, and I have seen him always respond with a loving spirit. He is a man of great love.

"I remember an incident on July 4, 1976, when Dr. Falwell probably made the greatest impression on me. A tremendous TV broadcast was being presented from Liberty Mountain. Dr. Falwell, Senator Byrd, and other dignitaries were on the platform. I was working as a security guard. One of the staff called me down from the platform and led me to a little old man on crutches. I walked up to him and he said, 'I've come so far, and I'll never be able to make this trip again. Do you think Dr. Falwell would have time to see me?' He went on to relate how much he enjoyed Dr. Falwell and the *Old-Time Gospel Hour* ministry. It was his heart's greatest desire just to meet the one whose ministry had meant so much to him. He wanted to shake Jerry's hand and meet him face to face.

"I went back to the platform and leaned down to Jerry, 'Jerry, there is an old man on crutches behind the platform. He's come a long way . . .' Before I could finish he was up and moving toward the back of the platform, down the back stairs toward the old man. Jerry reached out and took the old man's hand and put his arm around him. They talked as though they were two old friends. I saw the smile on the old man's face and the gleam in his eye. I thought of the immeasurable joy that must have filled his heart.

"God called my brother Mike and myself to Medford, Oregon, where we started Harvest Baptist Temple June 19, 1977. We left Lynchburg with a vision to win a city and a world to Christ. Our people have the same vision. Soul-winning is our first priority. People are being saved every week. Lives are being changed; families are being put back together. People are coming from every walk of life and finding Jesus Christ the Giver of Life. We expect to soon have more than four hundred in attendance every Sunday. We praise God for what He is doing and give Him all the glory for it . . . God used Jerry to instill in us a vision that will last a lifetime. He is a great man of God. The wonderful part about that is that he doesn't know it."

Chapter 15

A Church That Reaches Out

We give thanks to God always for you all . . . Remembering without ceasing your work of faith, and labour of love, and patience of hope in our Lord Jesus Christ (1 Thess. 1:2,3).

It is a Wednesday night in June. Most of the students of the Liberty Baptist Schools have returned to their homes for the summer vacation or are out on special assignment in churches or in various parts of the world mission field. In Lynchburg, however, it is prayer meeting night, and the Thomas Road Baptist Church sanctuary is packed with members of the congregation and visitors who have come from almost every region of the United States. Don Norman leads the audience in a hymn, while J. O. Grooms, the director of soul-winning at Thomas Road, glances at key Scripture verses in preparation to lead the congregation in a Scripture memorization lesson.

In a medium-sized room just off to the side of the platform, a group of junior-high aged young people are putting the final touches to "The Castaways," a puppet show based on the parable of the prodigal son. From his seat just to the left of the pulpit, Jim Moon, the church's co-pastor since 1968, looks out over the sanctuary to see if a young couple he has been counseling have fulfilled their promise to attend services. Then, as the last notes of the hymn are played, Jerry Falwell comes to the platform. During the course of this day, he has had to be businessman, counselor, mediator, teacher, organizer, and administrator, but now he will do what he most loves to do—he will minister the Word of God to his flock.

Jerry first calls the congregation's attention to the white prayer sheet they were given when they entered the sanctuary. This prayer sheet lists many general and special needs, beginning with several aspects of the Thomas Road program and the problems of its members. Someone is concerned about a new occupation; another is troubled by an extra financial crisis; one congregant is hopeful that his brother will evidence growth in Christ; a middle-aged couple seeks to know God's will for their lives. The list also includes a long series of names of those who are sick. Finally, the prayer list calls attention to a group of names who evidence the church's keen interest in evangelism. These are people to whom members of the church have been witnessing. Jerry asks the congregation to split into groups of three and spend several minutes in prayer.

Jerry Falwell often tells his congregation that prayer is vitally important. It is evident that Thomas Road is a praying church. Its members and friends know that their prayer requests will be prayed for specifically, by name, in a Friday morning prayer group, in a Wednesday night prayer meeting, in a daily staff devotion meeting, in a student prayer group, or in the homes of the hundreds of church members who commit themselves to pray daily for written prayer requests that are sent or given to the church.

"There is no limit to the power of prayer," says Jerry. "God loves His children and is concerned about every detail of their lives. God will answer our prayers—not always as we wish them answered, but always in accordance with His will and for our good. Jesus does all things well. Let us claim the promises of God through prayer. I am convinced that if we are to reach the world for Christ in this generation, we must train and mobilize a mighty army of praying people. The great movings of God in every generation have had their beginning in prayer meetings.''

''A great moving of God'' is what Jerry desires the church to be characterized by. ''Pray for the power of the Holy Spirit to be evidenced in every one of our ministries. If we could be doing what we are doing without prayer, we have no right doing any of it. I need your prayers,'' he tells the congregation at Thomas Road, ''I need them desperately as a pastor, as a preacher, and as a Christian leader. I feel the need of divine wisdom to know how to lead this ministry. I need the power of heaven upon my public speaking ministry. I need guidance as I attempt to lead these young people. Please lift my name to the throne of God daily in your prayers.''

Those who recall his early years in the ministry suggest that Jerry has gradually developed into a great preacher. Jerry has a unique philosophy about preaching and has not tried to model himself after anyone else. He believes that the principal requirement for preaching is to ''stay totally dependent upon God and trust God to flow through you. If you do this, His purpose will be accomplished; His Word will not return void. When a preacher gets to the place where he tries to entertain or impress people or magnify himself, he won't succeed.''

Falwell believes that to be effective as a preacher, a man must first feel a definite call from God. Otherwise, he will fade out after the initial glamour of the ministry has worn off. The man must have a real love for people and be willing to study.

As the congregation at Thomas Road is fed the Word of God, they in turn desire to reach out and minister to other people. Although described by major magazines as the nation's leading pastor of the "electronic church," Jerry's firm conviction is that the local, New Testament church is "God's sole agency for world evangelization."

When asked to describe the local church, Jerry replies, "The local church is very precious to God. It was taken from the pierced side of His Son, the Lord Jesus Christ. It is a body of born-again, baptized believers, banded together for the purpose of carrying out the Great Commission, which is three-fold. First, winning people to Jesus Christ is paramount. Second, baptizing them into the local church is commanded. Third, teaching them to live the Christian life which now is theirs and to become soul-winners themselves is likewise commanded. I believe every saved person should belong to that kind of local church. There he should give his time, his talent, and his treasure.

"The real mission of the New Testament church is to reach the world with the gospel of Jesus Christ. We are to begin at Jerusalem, but we are also to go on to the uttermost parts of the earth. God has given us a burden to start at least five thousand new churches on the North American continent in the next few years. We have asked God to plant literally hundreds of missionaries all over the planet who will likewise be establishing New Testament churches. The hope for our nation, and for the world, is in the establishment of local, New Testament churches that will reach and teach the people of our generation and mobilize them to participate in world evangelization."

Although Thomas Road now has sixteen thousand members, it is a growing church. "I sincerely believe the greatest days of Thomas Road Baptist Church are before us," Jerry says. "We will do whatever is possible and necessary to reach the world for Christ. I want us to be the greatest church since Pentecost, not for personal fame but for lost souls. Our only competition is . . . Satan. My eyes are not on those who run beside me; my eyes are on the goal.''

Thomas Road Baptist Church has many outreach ministries. Sunday services and classes are designed to relate to all age groups.

Everyone in Lynchburg and its surrounding communities has the opportunity to ride a church bus to the services. Thomas Road uses buses as an evangelistic tool, basing this activity on passages of Scripture, such as Luke 14:21,23, ''. . . Go out quickly into the streets and lanes of the city, and bring in hither the poor, and the maimed, and the halt, and the blind . . . Go out into the highways and hedges, and compel them to come in, that my house may be filled.''

The children's ministry specializes in providing spiritually sound programs and activities for all children. When just eighteen months old, children are taught God's Word. Underprivileged children who attend Sunday school are given special attention. In addition to the regular Sunday programs, children are ministered to through activities, athletics, Bible clubs, camps, evangelism, visitation, and Awana Bible and service clubs.

One Sunday morning while Dr. Hindson was teaching the pastor's Bible class, the junior department director asked Jerry Falwell to come up to see one of his fourth grade boys' classes. Jerry did not know who taught it, but he took former New York Yankee, Bobby Richardson, who was visiting Thomas Road that day, with him. The class of fourth grade boys was packed. The teacher, Dick Tate, had about eight or ten of the boys lined up in front of the class, and they were quoting the first chapter of John.

The boys quoted every word correctly and spoke perfectly in unison.

Later Jerry told Richardson Dick's story. Nine years before, Dick had been an alcoholic, and Jerry had met him in prison. Dick used to be a left-handed pitcher in the St. Louis Cardinal system. Now he was sixty years old. In the last nine years he had been teaching boys and girls things he did not know when he was their age. Relating tragic experiences in his life, he warned the children what the absence of Christ in their lives would do to them and what the presence of Christ in their lives could do for them. The children loved him.

When Jerry took Bobby to the airport, Bobby said, "You know, Jerry, the highlight of my whole trip was not that great banquet last night, as much as I enjoyed it. It wasn't being in those tremendous services this morning. It was your taking me over there to that fourth-grade class of boys, listening to those kids, looking at that dedicated teacher, and realizing the divine miracle that had taken place in his life. Then I thought about the thousands of other boys and girls in that building getting the same dedicated teaching those boys were getting. I walked away in awe."

Thomas Road Baptist Church has one of the most extensive local church youth ministries in the world. Hundreds of teenagers flock into the church's youth departments every Sunday. Dynamic programs are geared to meet their spiritual and social needs. They are "Youth Aflame," excited young people who are taught principles of soul-winning, separation, and discipline. As large, active, and aggressive as the Thomas Road Sunday school is, it forms only one part of a massive youth program that is operated on a seven-day-a-week basis.

The director of this program is Gordon Luff, a former

New Yorker who met Jerry Falwell after achieving considerable youth work success in California. Jerry first contacted Gordon Luff in the late 1960s and invited him to Lynchburg to discuss his vision for Lynchburg's young people. Gordon agreed to come, but he was skeptical since his experience with most pastors had proven them woefully inadequate in understanding the needs of youth. On their first weekend together, Gordon asked Jerry at least three hundred questions and ''got the right answer to each one.'' His initial reaction was that Jerry, unlike most pastors who had difficulty seeing beyond their own church, wanted to reach every one of the world's one billion teenagers. Gordon was impressed with Jerry. ''As we spent time in his office, in restaurants, and at his home that weekend, I was struck by three characteristics: Jerry's vision—his ability to see beyond present problems to a potentially successful outcome; his lack of pretense; and his love for people. You just couldn't get him to say anything negative about anyone.''

The youth program at Thomas Road is comprehensive enough to fill a teenager or young adult's entire week with activities. There are Monday night Bible studies that meet in units of twenty-five to thirty at local homes. On Wednesday night, each of the three youth departments conducts a midweek service, while Thursday and Friday evenings are given over to athletics and other activities. The church maintains leagues in all major sports. Instead of conducting a traditional Sunday school class on Sundays, each department holds its own rally with music and a speaker. There are always many activities. During Halloween week, ten thousand Lynchburg young people turn out for a ''Scare Mare'' activity (tour of a ''haunted'' house followed by a gospel presentation) put on by the young people of Thomas Road.

One of the reasons for the great success of Thomas Road in reaching people has been its intense concern for every person in the Lynchburg community. Every summer more than four thousand children enjoy a free camping experience on Treasure Island, the island Jerry saw and claimed for God. Senior citizens, or "senior saints" as these folks are affectionately referred to, are provided with five major programs. Plans have already been drawn for a retirement village on Liberty Mountain.

Thomas Road has a dynamic ministry to mentally retarded and handicapped people. Each week more than two hundred of these special people are brought by bus to attend four Sunday school classes. Liberty Baptist College is currently devising a special education major as part of its regular academic program, and the church's master plan calls for a home for the mentally retarded to be built on Liberty Mountain. Thomas Road also has a wide-ranging ministry for the deaf. Every service, class, and activity of the church and the Liberty Baptist Schools is interpreted for the deaf. Each week thousands of deaf persons across the nation are exposed to the gospel through the interpretation for the deaf that is an integral part of the *Old-Time Gospel Hour* TV program. Each year the counseling department of Thomas Road ministers personally to more than two thousand people.

Jerry Falwell loves people, and the church he pastors has been led to be a loving and giving church. A man named Bob Grimsley wrote,

Dear Dr. Falwell: Approximately four years ago, my wife and I were transferred to the Lynchburg area with the intention of a short business stay. Both of us had church backgrounds as children but were a long way from God's plan for our lives. As a result of the work that God has entrusted to you, several Liberty Baptist College students, their testimonies and God putting us in contact with them, resulted in our knowing the saving grace of Jesus Christ. On May 14, 1976, we attended a Liberty Baptist graduation service, and for the first time to our knowledge, heard why Jesus died and rose again. Dr. Harold Willmington very patiently dealt with my wife and me that evening, and we were both saved. Our lives have been changed drastically from that time to now. God has worked miracle after miracle, changed our direction and the purpose of our lives. This letter is to in some way say "thank you" for your devotion and dedication, to thank the church and those supporting the school. . . .

Each year the Thomas Road Baptist Church hosts many conferences intended to help and inspire thousands of people who come to Lynchburg for these special sessions. Conferences such as the Super Conference, the Youth Conference, and the Pastoral Counseling Institute motivate multitudes of people. After attending the Super Conference, one pastor testified, "I have been in the ministry for eleven years and almost felt at times like I was slowly starving to death. This conference has been the greatest spiritual feast I have had since I was saved fourteen years ago."

The total ministry of the Thomas Road Baptist Church is farflung and highly ambitious and as such cannot be operated without proper financing or implemented without competent staff. In 1979 the Thomas Road Baptist Church and Liberty Baptist Schools employed more than eight hundred full-time staff and faculty members. Financial resources for the Jerry Falwell Ministries are received through two basic means. These come internally through the tithes and offerings of the church's members, and externally through the gifts sent in by the *Old-Time Gospel Hour* audience.

The costs of the television and radio ministries alone are phenomenal, amounting to many millions of dollars each year. Jerry must spend much time presenting the needs to God's people and then trusting God to supply the needed funds. The Thomas Road family is well aware of the fact that Jerry never lets a missionary or visiting Christian worker in financial need leave Thomas Road Baptist Church without a substantial offering, no matter how serious are the church's needs at the time.

With ministries as extensive as those of Thomas Road, it is no wonder that there is a continual crisis situation with regard to finance. "God knows how to keep us daily and hourly abiding," says Jerry. "We pray for every dollar. We trust God and then thank Him daily for His blessings that never fail to come just in time. We have stepped out in faith to do great things for God. We have been driven to be prayer warriors, to trust God more, to launch out into the deep and let down our nets for a draught. Every day we have monumental needs because we are doing something for God. We would be out of the will of God if we had a fat bank account."

Jerry teaches the biblical principle of giving God the first ten percent of one's total income. He believes that a Christian's first obligation in tithing is to give to his local congregation. This he says does not mean a person should not contribute to the work of outside ministries. "Many of our people support evangelists and others preaching the Word of God. I do the same," Jerry remarks, "But we ask our people to give to them over and above their regular tithing to their own church. No one has given sacrificially until he has gone beyond ten percent. The tithe is a matter of how much you love the Lord. It is a matter of what life is all about. When people really get their hearts wrapped up in winning souls and winning the world for Jesus, they will start thinking of how much they can give to the Lord.''

The whole of Christianity is giving. One year the Thomas Road Baptist Church adopted as their theme verse Luke 6:38, "Give, and it shall be given unto you; good measure, pressed down, and shaken together, and running over, shall men give into your bosom. For with the same measure that ye mete withal it shall be measured to you again.'' As thousands of members gave sacrificially, they learned that God will be no man's debtor. Each found that God gave back to them far more than they had given.

Recently, Alvin Dark, a famous baseball player and manager sent in a check for one thousand dollars to Thomas Road Baptist Church. Enclosed was a note, ''Jerry, I have joined every club you have. Here is a check for the next one you start! I consider it a great privilege to be a part of the great work Thomas Road Baptist Church is doing for God.''

Chapter 16

Heartbeat For The World

And he said unto them, Go ye into all the world, and preach the gospel to every creature (Mark 16:15).

At 3:02 A.M., February 4, 1976, one of the worst tragedies ever to occur in the Western Hemisphere struck. The earthquake measured 7.5 on the Richter scale and was felt with varying intensities over a 2,200 mile swath from Mexico to Panama. During the forty seconds the earth shook in a violent convulsion, more than $400 million worth of damage was done to the Central American country of Guatemala, the home of six million people. The death toll from the earthquake was 23,000, with 6,000 people listed in critical condition and 90,000 injured. Many of the small towns in Guatemala were totally devastated. Unreinforced adobe dwellings dissolved into heaps of broken blocks and twisted beams under which sleeping occupants were buried. Hundreds of landslides blocked roads and isolated stricken villages.

Jerry Falwell called upon the members of Thomas Road Baptist Church and the listeners of the *Old-Time Gospel Hour* to come to the assistance of the earthquake victims. "It is our hour of opportunity. Let us pray for these people. Let us trust God for the funds to help them, and then let us go and suffer with our brothers and sisters in Christ in Guatemala and help them."

Like an army convoy, seven vehicles of SMITE

(Student Missionary Intern Training for Evangelism) campaigners rolled from the Thomas Road Baptist Church parking lot in the gray predawn hours of May 18. The group's destination: earthquake-shattered Guatemala. Their mission: to rebuild ten churches in one month.

From the first day of preparations for the campaign everyone knew it would be a tough job. But no one knew how formidable the obstacles would be. After seven tiring days of travel from Virginia's Blue Ridge mountains, through six states, across the border, and down the length of Mexico, the dust-covered trucks and vans finally entered Guatemala's cool climate. It was a welcome relief from the torrid Mexican heat, but it was also the beginning of a more exhausting experience.

Seven bulky army tents were unloaded from a SMITE van and a campsite was established. Makeshift tables and benches formed a kitchen. While countless Christians across America and Canada prayed for the project, the reconstruction progressed steadily. At times, it seemed that the work would not be completed on the unbelievable schedule of one church every three days. The obstacles were overwhelming. Besides the limitations of time and manpower, the group encountered difficulty transporting workers and supplies over the rugged, mountainous terrain. The daily rains made many roads impassable; others were already severely damaged by the earthquake. Some nights the temperature would drop into the low forties, and the students sleeping in tents could not keep warm. Some of the worksites in the remote highlands were accessible only on foot. Communication was also a constant difficulty. Three languages, English, Spanish, and Cakchiquel, the local Indian dialect, were spoken. But against the odds, the work continued. Guatemalan Christians joined the SMITE campaigners and worked diligently.

By the end of the summer, more than four hundred Liberty Baptist College student volunteers had been involved in the reconstruction mission. Ten churches had been reconstructed, more than twenty thousand New Testaments and Scripture portions, printed in Spanish and Cakchiquel, had been distributed, and hundreds of evangelistic services and concerts had been conducted in cities throughout Guatemala. Joyous services had been conducted in the newly constructed buildings. Another mission of love and compassion had been performed.

From its earliest days, the Thomas Road Church has supported missionaries. Jerry sees the church's primary task as world evangelization. "There are 4.4 billion people living in our world today," he tells his congregation and the listeners of the *Old-Time Gospel Hour*. "Jesus Christ died for every one of the people who are alive today. I believe that we have an obligation to meet the physical needs of a hungry and hurting world, but this is secondary. I believe we need to commit ourselves to correcting the moral and political inequities of our society, but this too must be secondary. Our major and primary task is the same one our Lord gave to his disciples, 'preach the gospel to every creature.' God has given us a clear command, 'Go, tell, make disciples.' We must never become insensitive to God's call to take the message of God's redeeming grace, through the death, burial, and resurrection of Jesus Christ, to the ends of the earth."

In recent years Jerry has developed an increasing world vision. He and Roscoe Brewer, mission's director of Thomas Road, spend much time in prayer and careful examination of foreign fields. In an attempt to consolidate its overseas outreach, Thomas Road established Strategic Baptist Missions, an agency designed to reach key fields of the world. In implementing its program, Thomas Road's Strategic Baptist Missions uses the church's highly effective SMITE teams as its spearhead. Roscoe Brewer founded the concept of SMITE and developed this unique program while a youth pastor in Tulsa, Oklahoma. Roscoe first tried out the SMITE approach in Mexico, and today there are missionaries serving on every continent as a result of SMITE. Thomas Road has five SMITE teams, each with its own geographical and programmatic emphasis. During the school year, the SMITE teams travel by bus each weekend to churches and present the needs of the foreign field by use of a multi-media program. During school vacations, the teams travel overseas. Each member of the team is responsible for raising his own travel and maintenance expenses. While out on the mission field, the team works through, and in cooperation with, local missionaries. The local church is both the goal and the means of reaching the world.

Since the organization of the first SMITE team soon after LBC's founding, Jerry has sent them to conduct evangelistic crusades in hundreds of foreign countries on every continent. During the summer of 1977, LBC students traveled in the Orient, Australia, New Zealand, and Brazil, and continued the outreach in Mexico. They ministered in local churches, high school assemblies, outdoor concerts, military institutions, youth camps, prisons, hospitals, and on foreign radio and television stations. Some of the teams visited mission churches organized by graduates of the Liberty Baptist Schools. One team held a special concert in the Korean National Theatre before two thousand government dignitaries. This was the first time a Christian group had performed in the prestigious concert hall. Thousands of Bibles were distributed by the concerned students of Liberty Baptist College.

On August 19, 1977, Jerry Falwell, Roscoe Brewer, Sumner Wemp, a photographer, and two pilots went to Haiti at the invitation of Antoine Alexis, a native Haitian and recent graduate of Liberty Baptist College. These men were shocked by what they saw. As the result of a serious drought, Haitian people had many desperate needs. Upon returning from the trip Jerry said, "My heart is broken. Seven million people are starving, physically and spiritually." Jerry had preached in Haiti, and Antoine had interpreted. He had watched the people listen hungrily to the gospel message. He was determined to help them.

"While the primary responsibility of the church and the Christian is to meet the spiritual needs of its generation, we must be concerned about the world's physical and emotional needs as well," Jerry told his Lynchburg congregation. "James warns us against offering our blessings to people in a spiritual sense when we know they are hungry and we do nothing about it. We as Christians must realize that God loves people and 'is touched with the feelings of their infirmities.' God is not impressed with buildings and budgets and programs. He is impressed with people. Let us become involved in relieving the aches and the pains of a world in turmoil. 1 John 3:17 asks us, 'But whoso hath this world's good, and seeth his brother have need, and shutteth up his bowels of compassion from him, how dwelleth the love of God in him?' Our own needs are great at this time, but this must not stop us from doing what God would have us do. We must just trust Him a little more."

The most extensive work on the island of Haiti has been done by Wallace and Eleanor Turnbull who launched a Baptist mission work there in 1946. Their work encompasses 134 indigenous churches, 127 Christian day schools, a 100-bed hospital, youth camps, and a multiplicity of self-help programs. When Jerry Falwell said he would send help to Haiti, Antoine Alexis joined forces with the Turnbulls in the organization of the help that was to come. Antoine is now the superintendent of a work comprised of twenty-four churches. He is also co-pastor of White Rock Baptist Church in St. Marc, a town of 150,000. The White Rock Church operates a Christian school with an enrollment of six hundred students and has recently opened a Bible institute. The goal of the institute is to train national leaders to establish local churches. Antoine, who is described by Jerry as "a man of vision," plans to establish an orphanage and a medical clinic.

Soon after his trip, Jerry developed an immediate and a long-range program to meet the nation's needs. "We cannot be indifferent to the great distress in Haiti," he said. "God opened the doors that we might see the needs there. Our Haitian brothers, co-laborers in the gospel, know the real meaning of sacrifice. They are men who know the power of the Holy Spirit in their lives. God is calling us to help our brothers reach lost multitudes on an island in desperate need of the Lord Jesus Christ."

Soon "Project Haiti" was under way. More than 175 LBC young people gave up their Christmas vacation to work in Haiti. At the close of a three-week effort, two schools and a dormitory had been constructed, a food distribution program had been initiated, and twenty-five evangelistic services had been conducted in local churches on the island. Numerous Bible lessons had been taught in homes and open markets. The Christmas campaign was climaxed when more than eight thousand people attended a rally in the city stadium in Port-au-Prince where the gospel was presented in music and testimony by the SMITE Singers.

Monumental needs have been met in Haiti, and the project still continues today. A year after the project was begun, Thomas Road Baptist Church was responsible for the construction of two elementary Christian schools that accommodate up to fifteen hundred students. Under the leadership of Wallace and Eleanor Turnbull, Baptist Haiti Missions, a concrete block dormitory had been constructed at a youth camp. Students from Liberty Baptist Schools had completely wired the vocational school where Antoine Alexis works under Strategic Baptist Missions in Haiti.

Twenty-five students from the Liberty Baptist Schools returned to Haiti during their Easter break and worked in construction. Another larger group followed up. Several couples from the Thomas Road Baptist Church responded to the need for workers in Haiti. A full-time missions staff member of Thomas Road served for many months coordinating the Haiti project.

The Thomas Road Baptist Church continues to send $12,000 in monthly support to missionaries and missionary enterprises in Haiti. In the last year crops have been coming up well in Haiti. It is the first time in six years there has been adequate rain. Missionaries continue to work hard preaching the gospel and teaching people how to make a living for their families.

In discussing the most significant world problems, Jerry told an interviewer, "The number one problem in the world today is, without question, communism. Communism is godlessness and is, of course, anti-Christ. The number one objective of communism is world conquest. This has never changed from the very inception of Marxism. In the sixty-two years since the Bolshevik Revolution of 1917, a major portion of the world has been engulfed in this political sickness.''

During the summer of 1978 gospel teams from LBC presented the gospel on four continents. The different teams each conducted four and five concerts daily, and a total of thirty-four thousand professions of faith were recorded.

Two teams concentrated their efforts in Asia and the South Pacific. The LBC Chorale, under the direction of Gordon Luff, conducted fifty-one programs in fifteen days in five major cities in South Korea. More than 16,500 professions of faith were recorded. Roscoe Brewer led the SMITE Singers in twenty-six services there in nine days and witnessed 6,100 professions of faith in Jesus Christ.

While they ministered, Thomas Road Baptist Church prayed for the groups and raised money to make their crusades possible. Jerry relayed their progress to the Thomas Road family. ''Our young people ministering in Korea say it is the most pro-American, pro-Christian country in the world. At one school, a thousand students lined the entrance road, waving American flags. The mayors and public officials of every city in which the teams appear are giving them their full cooperation. South Koreans are fearful. The thirty-eighth parallel is only one hour away from them by car. There is a tense atmosphere in South Korea. Their officials agree that if American troops withdraw from South Korea, the North Koreans will, without question, invade, supported by Russia or China. South Korea cannot defend herself. Christians will be the first to die. Many estimate that as many as six million Christians could be killed. Our students are ministering with a sense of urgency. They rise early each morning. They ride on hot buses and eat on the run. They get little sleep, and all this after having had to raise part of their own support. This is our second summer in Korea. We must continue to pray for Korea and for our brothers and sisters in Christ there.''

After seeing the needs on foreign fields, many of the Liberty team members have pledged themselves to return to give their lives in overseas ministries. After ministering in Korea, Joe and Ann Hale, graduates of LBC, returned to Korea to lead a youth ministry at the Central Baptist Church in Suwon, South Korea. Rick Sirico returned to Adelaide, Australia, to be a youth pastor at Prospect Baptist Church. These young people are supported by Thomas Road Baptist Church. Few know of the hundreds of thousands of dollars that are spent yearly in taking the gospel to the world. Only eternity will reveal what a precious expenditure of money it is.

Recently, Larry Ward of Food for the Hungry, International, visited Jerry in Lynchburg. He shared with him the plight of 130,000 refugees in northern Thailand who are located in thirteen camps. Ward told Jerry about the unbelievable atrocities that have occurred since the United States withdrew its military forces from Southeast Asia. He told how the Communists had slaughtered between two and three million men, women, and children. This occurred primarily in Cambodia, but also in Vietnam and Laos. The 130,000 refugees in Thailand had fled there. Most of them had crossed the Mekong River from Laos.

Roscoe Brewer and his team went to Thailand and returned to relate stories of bravery, coupled with tragedy, that abound in the refugee camps of northern Thailand.

One such story is of a twelve-year-old boy named Vang Kong and his family who came from a small village in Laos. The entire village of three hundred was made up of

Christians. When the Communists took over Laos, they announced that only twenty percent of the people in a village could profess Christianity. Vang Kong and his family learned that many people in a neighboring village were slaughtered. Vang's father went to the border to seek a way of escape for his family and was shot there. Vang's mother took him and his brother to the Mekong River which separates Communist Laos from free Thailand. The Mekong River is a treacherous river, approximately a quarter of a mile wide. There Vang's mother tied his baby brother, only a few months old, to Vang's back. Vang plunged into the water. His mother tried to swim across the river but did not make it. She was arrested by the Communists. Vang made it across the river and now resides in a refugee camp in northern Thailand. He does not know what became of his mother. Roscoe and his team talked to Vang and to hundreds of other refugees. They heard about the countless thousands who died before reaching freedom. "Freedom" is a packed refugee camp.

As he listened to the heartbreaking reports, Jerry knew he must immediately get involved. During the Christmas holidays, a SMITE team of twenty ministered in the refugee camps and worked on a "mercy" ship in the South China Sea, aiding fleeing refugees headed for other shores. They fed twenty-seven thousand refugees, gave out ten thousand blankets, ten thousand Bibles, and more than forty thousand toys. The gospel was preached, tracts were passed out, and the SMITE team sang in the language of the people. Desperate people were given a message of hope. The gifts were all presented in Jesus' name.

Roscoe Brewer wrote in his journal,

In the early morning light of dawn, January 9, 1979, I looked into the faces of eighty-eight Vietnamese refugees, loaded into a flimsy boat, floating without fuel in the middle of the South China Sea. At first they were afraid that we were going to harm them.

I had read the articles about the ''boat people'' and seen the newscasts about these victims who were fleeing Communist persecution. The newscasts had shown starving, desperate people. One group had been attacked by pirates and the men killed and the women raped. All of the ''boat people'' had unbelievable needs.

We yelled over the loud speaker in Vietnamese, 'Good News!' They began cheering because that was a familiar Christian greeting. They brought their small craft alongside our ship.

At first the entire project seemed strange to me because I had been interested in planting churches all over the world. Saving lives seemed far removed from the goal. But then you can't plant a church among dead people. Over 50,000 of the boat people have drowned or perished at sea in recent months. The *Far Eastern Economic Review* estimates another 200,000 will try to escape before this summer. I am distressed because the authorities estimate half of these will not make it. Who in the world will really care about them if Christians don't?

I was on the Bamboo Cross, a mercy ship owned by Food For The Hungry, International, that was outfitted by the gifts from the viewers of the *Old-Time Gospel Hour*. As we got ready to leave, the steam boiler developed a leak. It took the students and me two days in the boilers to repair them. But it was all worth it when I stood on deck and saw that first boat overflowing with people.

I saw a boy about eleven years old reach out to me.

I saw a man hold up empty cups because they were out of water. I saw their little boat tossing aimlessly in the heavy sea because they were out of fuel.

I saw a tiny baby who needed milk. There was a woman who would soon give birth.

As I passed plastic bags of supplies into that little boat,

the people applauded. One woman cried. She was a Christian who had prayed that help would come. We gave them fresh water, food, Bibles, and fuel. It was so obvious they were thankful and could sense our love.

I knew as a Christian I had a responsibility to help save lives. I wanted to take them on the Bamboo Cross and get them to a safe place. But we were not allowed to pick them up, so we did all we could. We gave them supplies for ten days and a compass, then gave them directions to a friendly port. I prayed they would all somehow make it to safety.

While the refugee boat was alongside ours, our Filipino cook pushed his way to the rail and carefully looked at each refugee, then sadly turned away. He had married a Vietnamese girl and had not seen her for five years. "Maybe next time," he said.

There will be thousands more of other desperate refugees in little boats who will need help. The Bamboo Cross must be there to help them in Jesus' name. The "boat people" need our help now!

Jerry's long-range plans are to relocate many of the refugee families in South America. Several South American countries have given hundreds of square miles for resettlement. Since the climate and land conditions are similar to those in Southeast Asia, the refugees, who are farmers by tradition, can quickly become self-supporting. Churches can be planted and evangelism accomplished.

Jerry's eyes are on the world. As he continues to preach about dedication, surrender, abandonment to the will of God, and obsession with a message and a mission, hundreds more will go out from the Thomas Road Baptist Church and the Liberty Baptist Schools filled with a compassion for people to take the gospel of Jesus Christ to the ends of the earth.

Chapter 17

One Common Goal

. . . walk worthy of the vocation wherewith ye are called, With all lowliness and meekness, with longsuffering, forebearing one another in love; Endeavoring to keep the unity of the Spirit in the bond of peace (Eph. 4:1–3).

Alon Moreh is a town so tiny it doesn't appear on most current maps of Israel. In fact, Alon Moreh is not really a town at all but a settlement established in 1975 by a small band of patriotic and determined Israelis who fervently believe that Judea and Samaria belong by biblical and historical right to the Jewish people.

On a windy, cool but brilliantly sunny late November afternoon in 1978, Jerry Falwell visited the settlement to meet with its inhabitants and interview several of them for a television special he was preparing on modern-day Israel. Prior to his trip to Alon Moreh, Jerry had met with Prime Minister Menachem Begin in his office to discuss important matters concerning Israel and peace in the Middle East. Jerry had also met with Prime Minister Begin and Egyptian President Anwar Sadat in April of that year.

Now as he visited Alon Moreh, Jerry met and talked with young Jed Atlas, a transplanted American businessman who two years before had made the decision to leave his home in Cherry Hill, New Jersey, to live in the ancient Jewish homeland. Jed, a serious-minded student of the Scriptures and a practicing Orthodox Jew, sat with Jerry in the small house trailer he calls home and with open Bible in hand showed Jerry the passage in Genesis that mentioned the site of the modern-day Alon Moreh settlement. Jerry was much taken with the young man and with his zeal and determination. He was equally impressed with all the inhabitants of the settlement he met that day.

After leaving Jed Atlas, Jerry walked down the steep hill to the small, neat, flower-filled house of Daniella Weiss, a young Jewish mother who was one of the first inhabitants of the settlement. Daniella told Jerry of the trials and tribulations of establishing a community and how the original founders had started down at the bottom of the hill about two miles away near an abandoned railroad station. At first, they had no running water, electricity, or heat, and they lived in tents and crude shacks. Later the settlers were able to build a community, which has now become economically and socially viable though in danger politically of losing its status as a result of recent Middle East peace discussions. Jerry was tremendously moved by Daniella's story. As the two went outside to look over at the nearby hills that the settlers hope will someday also be populated by Jews from around the world, Jerry became silent and meditated.

As he stood in the biting wind and swirling dust of Alon Moreh, he recalled both the promise God made to Abraham and its confirmation articulated by the apostle Paul in the ninth chapter of Romans. God told Abraham in Genesis 12:3 that "I will bless them that bless thee, and curse him that curseth thee. . ." Jerry thought of how history is replete with examples of God's fulfillment of this dual promise of blessing and cursing. He thought about the Jewish nation as special to God and the land of Israel as God's chosen land. He thought with anticipation of the day when civilization, which had begun on that sacred spot, would consummate there.

The continuing Middle East conflict is a crucial political issue that deeply concerns Jerry Falwell. He frequently addresses this world problem, taking the Bible as his starting point. "Since America has been kind to the Jew, God has been kind to America," Jerry preaches, "The Christian must politically involve himself in such a way as to guarantee that America continues to be a friend of the Jew. In recent years, there have been incidents at the very highest levels that would indicate that America is wavering at this time in her position on the side of Israel. I believe that if we fail to protect Israel, we will cease to be important to God. For the Christian, political involvement in this issue is not only a right, but a responsibility. We can and must be involved in guiding America towards a biblical position regarding her stand on Israel. Psalm 122:6 tells us, 'Pray for the peace of Jerusalem: they shall prosper that love thee.' "

Jerry's trip to the Middle East in April of 1978 was made at the invitation of the Egyptian and Israeli governments who sponsored and paid for the trip. Jerry and a chosen group of evangelical leaders from the United States communicated their feelings regarding a peace settlement in the Middle East to Egyptian President Anwar Sadat, Israeli Prime Minister Menachem Begin, and many heads of state. As spokesman for the group, Jerry related what the Bible says concerning the future of Egypt and Israel. He spoke of his desire to see both countries be completely open to gospel preaching and church building.

Each of the evangelical leaders who participated in the Middle East trip represented mainline religious denominations in the United States. Jerry Falwell represented fundamentalism. There was a day when the word "fundamentalist" had a bad connotation. Jerry Falwell is a fundamentalist, but he does not separate himself from good Christian men simply because they do not agree with him on every detail of theological discussion. He says, "I am a friend of those who are friends of Christ."

On the first Sunday of 1979, Jerry announced that it was "Commitment Day." "First," began Jerry, "we are freshly committing ourselves to the Word of God and to the articles of faith, the doctrinal stand on which the church of the living God was established two thousand years ago—the faith of our fathers. Secondly, we are making a commitment to the lordship of Christ in our lives. We believe that the key to victorious Christian living is putting Jesus Christ first in our lives. Thirdly, we are freshly committing ourselves to world evangelization, getting the gospel out to the world in our generation."

Hundreds of people left their seats that morning at Thomas Road and slowly made their way to the front of the church. They knelt all across the front and filled the aisles. Thousands of voices repeated together:

We believe in the verbal inspiration and absolute infallibility of the Scriptures. We believe that the Bible reveals God, the fall of man, the way of salvation, and God's plan and purpose in the ages. We believe in God the Father, God the Son, and God the Holy Spirit. We believe in the diety and virgin birth of Jesus Christ. We believe that salvation is "by grace," plus nothing and minus nothing. The conditions to salvation are repentance and faith. We believe that men are justified by faith alone and are accounted righteous before God only through the merit of our Lord and Savior Jesus Christ who was crucified, buried, and resurrected from the dead to effect our salvation. We believe in the visible, personal, and premillennial return of Jesus Christ. We believe in the everlasting conscious blessedness of the saved and the everlasting conscious punishment of the lost. We believe that Christians, by the aid of the Holy Spirit, should walk together in Christian love, should lead lives that are characterized by holy and righteous living, should walk circumspectly in the world, being exemplary in our deportment, and separated in our habits.

Then Jerry Falwell prayed, "Our Heavenly Father, in the precious name of the Lord Jesus we ask You right now to take these words that we have spoken and register them in heaven. They come as convictions from our hearts; we believe what we have said. We want Jesus to be the Lord of all in our lives. We want Him to be our King. We want His Word to be our Guidebook for life. We want to deliver this message, this faith of our fathers to the world. We ask this in Jesus' name."

These are the priorities that Jerry Falwell has established at the Thomas Road Baptist Church and the Liberty Baptist Schools. Jerry is dogmatic as he insists, "I don't know how long the Lord is going to allow me to live. If the Lord hasn't come yet, and some of you outlive me, I want you to know that if this church and these schools ever stand for something besides what we have just stood for today, they should be burned to the ground.

"I am a fundamentalist and a separatist. I serve on various committees with other fundamentalists and separatists. I often preach in their pulpits and they in mine. We work together, pray together, plan together, and live in close proximity to one another. Some things we do not agree on. Our preferences are a little different in some areas. However, we do agree on the inspiration of Scripture, the deity of the Son of God, His virgin birth, His sinless life, His vicarious death, His glorious resurrection, and His imminent return. We believe in the power that is in the blood of Jesus. We believe that every man of the world is lost without a work of divine regeneration in his heart. We believe in building great soul-winning churches.

"It is time fundamentalists and separatists learned to be gentlemen. It is time we allowed others to think, preach, and write whatever they please and love one another in spite of it. It is time fundamentalists and separatists learned to be brethren and do the job together.

"It seems that Satan is working overtime to divide the brethren today. There are many reasons for this. Obviously, it is to the advantage of Satan to separate us. If we believers spend all of our time fighting each other, we will have little time to do combat with Satan. Beyond that, Satan likewise enjoys the injury that is done to our testimony before a lost world when we saints appear to be stabbing each other in the back. Public warfare among Christian leaders and Christian ministries is great opportunity for unbelievers everywhere to blame the gospel and excuse themselves for their own renunciation of the faith we embrace.

"It is right to go to war over biblical truth. It is pleasing to the Lord for His children to stand firm for the faith once delivered. There are many today who call themselves fundamentalists and separatists but who have long since departed our ranks. These people need to be exposed. Many of the schools and churches that were once true to God have gone into liberalism. Very few seminaries in America today are totally true to the inspiration of Scripture and the cardinal doctrines of the Word of God. For that reason, Thomas Road Baptist Church is not affiliated with any earthly organization. As a pastor, I find it impossible to financially support any program that, in turn, supports liberal professors and instructors in theological schools. To support apostates is totally contradictory to everything we stand for and believe. Here at Liberty Baptist College, every professor, instructor, administrator, and staff member must subscribe to the articles of faith before he or she is employed. If, during their employment, they depart from this declaration of faith, they are immediately dismissed. I could not, in good conscience, ask my friends across America to financially support this school if a professor or employee were receiving payment for teaching and representing heresy. The Board of Trustees of Liberty Baptist College is charged with the responsibility of keeping this institution pure. We must always publicly and openly take our stand for truth and against error.

"Likewise, it is the obligation and responsibility of Christian leaders to stand openly against worldliness and modernism. We feel an obligation to declare our stand against the manufacture, sale, and consumption of alcoholic beverages to any degree. We believe the Bible teaches 'teetotalism.' We believe that we must take our open stand against religious organizations that are publishing liberal and modernistic material for distribution among the people of God. We believe we have an obligation to openly cry out against liberalism when it creeps into our colleges, seminaries, and churches.

"However, on the world scene much division among religious leaders is being predicated upon 'personal preferences' rather than 'scriptural convictions.' For example, here at Liberty Baptist College, we require the boys to keep their hair cut rather short. We do not allow the hair to touch the collar in the back, the ears on the side, or to fall into the region of the eyes in front. Admittedly, we have no Scripture to tell us what is the proper length for boys' hair. We do know from 1 Corinthians 11:14 that boys' hair should not be long. The Scripture reference here is designed to prevent boys from looking effeminate. The man is to be the leader in the home and in the church. At no time is he to appear woman-like. We do not know 'how long is long.' However, our particular rule on hair length at Liberty Baptist College is based upon preference and the ease with which we can enforce the rule. It is easier for us to enforce a rule that has the limitations which we have determined. However, we do not believe that hair length and spirituality are synonymous.

"When I started in the ministry twenty-seven years ago I believed that the Bible—every word of it—was the inspired Word of God. I believed that Jesus died upon the cross for all men and that all men could and should be saved. I believed that God had saved me to tell the world about His death, His burial, and His resurrection. I believe exactly the same way today. If I am living twenty-seven years from now, and the Lord has not come, I will still be believing and preaching that same message! Even then I am sure there will be those who will want to tell us who should and should not preach for us, where we should and should not preach, and even who we should and should not eat with! But we are determined to keep on winning souls, building young people in the faith of our Lord Jesus Christ, and capturing cities and a world for Christ. We had better forget that we are not all in the same organization! I am a friend to all who are friends of Christ. I want to be that way for the rest of my life. Let us unite and win the victory together!"

Today Jerry and the Thomas Road Baptist Church are engaged in an interesting and exciting curriculum experiment. Jerry has joined with three outstanding preachers, Dr. Truman Dollar, pastor of Kansas City Baptist Temple, Dr. A. V. Henderson, pastor of the Temple Baptist

Church, Detroit, and Dr. Jack Hyles, pastor of the First Baptist Church, Hammond, Indiana, the church with the world's largest Sunday school. Together these men are editing a series of Sunday school materials. This curriculum is made available to the church by Fundamentalist Church Publications, and includes both student and teacher manuals. The lessons prepared by Jerry and his colleagues are not meant to replace, but rather to complement the normative work of the local fundamentalist church's Sunday school.

One of the most interesting aspects of the development of this new curriculum is its demonstration of unity among the editors. Although the primary purpose of Fundamentalist Church Publications is to provide a scripturally based Sunday school curriculum, it may also achieve a much-needed spirit of agreement and cooperation within the fundamentalist community, as the statement of purpose underlying the series suggests. "When two are in agreement, there can be walking together and working together. The members of the editorial committee are seeking to encourage fundamentalists, by their own experience, to cooperate with one another in the task of reaching the world for Christ. Their aim is to create a spirit of agreement so that there can be a united front in the fight against wickedness."

Love for people has made Jerry Falwell a big man and a true fundamentalist. There will always be those who will criticize him and the Thomas Road ministry, but in keeping with his priorities Jerry does not often respond to critics. Only if the criticism comes from a sincere person does he try to explain and be reconciled. His time is filled with reaching out to a world of 4.4 billion people—people for whom Christ died.

Chapter 18

Righteousness Exalteth A Nation

Righteousness exalteth a nation: but sin is a reproach to any people (Prov. 14:34).

Thousands of supporters of Jerry Falwell Ministries received an urgent letter in the spring of 1979.

April 30, 1979
Dear Friend:

My heart is burning within me today. It is about time that Christians here in America stand up and be counted for Jesus Christ. We are the "moral majority," and we have been silent long enough!

I realize that it is "popular" to be a born-again Christian. But for some strange reason it is "unpopular" to stand up and fight against the sins of our nation. Will you take a stand and help me Clean Up America? How would you answer these questions: Do you approve of pornographic and obscene classroom textbooks being used under the guise of sex education? Do you approve of the present laws legalizing abortion-on-demand that resulted in the murder of more than one million babies last year? Do you approve of the growing trend towards sex and violence replacing family-oriented programs on television?

If you are against these sins, then you are exactly the person I want on my team. I have put together a Clean Up America campaign that is going to shake this nation like it has never been shaken before. I cannot do it alone. Together we must awaken the moral conscience of our nation. The battle has just begun.

I am going to send ballots with the three questions I asked you in this letter to two million friends like you. Then special ballot ads will be run in the major magazines across America. The results from these ballots will be tabulated and sent to each and every lawmaker, state legislator, governor, U.S. senator and representative, judge, school board, P.T.A. president, TV network, the fifty major advertisers in the country, and to President Carter himself. I am devoting the entire month of May to Clean Up America. Every week, on television and radio, I will preach on a different sin our nation is committing. On May 27 we will televise on the *Old-Time Gospel Hour* the Clean Up America Rally we held on the steps of our nation's Capitol on April 27. And finally, throughout the coming year, I will appear on talk shows and campaign across the country supporting programs to Clean Up America.

It will cost us hundreds of thousands of dollars to accomplish these ends, but we must do it. If we do not accomplish the task, I am afraid that America will face the judgment of God. Proverbs 14:34 says, 'Righteousness exalteth a nation: but sin is a reproach to any people.' There is no way to escape this biblical fact. We do not have a moment to lose!

This year's campaign goals are to reverse the current trend towards uncensored sex and violence on television which are replacing family-oriented programs, to remove pornographic and obscene classroom textbooks (placed in the hand of minors under the guise of sex education) from the classrooms of America, and to stop the wholesale slaughter of unborn babies caused by legalized abortion. It is vital that you cast your vote to "Clean Up America" today! If several million concerned individuals will start praying and working to Clean Up America, and if hundreds of groups and churches work together, we will be able to bring this nation back to her moral senses. Only then can God once more bless our republic.

Yours in Christ,

Jerry Falwell

Twelve thousand people joined Falwell that April day when he launched his 1979 Clean Up America campaign from the steps of the U.S. Capitol Building. They gathered slowly in the pelting rain that day, some arriving four hours before the rally began. They came in cars, in vans, and in buses, from as far south as Florida and as far north as New York. Entire student bodies, along with hundreds of pastors and school principals were present. Reporters from the major networks and newspapers filtered through the crowds. As the rally began the rain stopped and the sun shone brilliantly.

The Clean Up America rally launched that day was the second of such campaigns Falwell had spearheaded in the last year. The theme of "Cleaning Up America" occupied a considerable amount of Jerry's time and energy during 1978. In May he launched a full-fledged campaign aimed at the three highly controversial public issues of abortion-on-demand, homosexuality, and pornography. By the end of the campaign, more than one million ballots, representing more than one million American homes, had flooded the offices of the *Old-Time Gospel Hour*. The response was 95.8 percent of the voters voted "no" to the questions: Do you approve of known practicing homosexuals teaching in public schools? Do you approve of the present laws legalizing abortion-on-demand? Do you approve of the laws of our land permitting the open display of pornographic materials on newsstands, TV, and movies? The results of the campaign were forwarded to the media and to every U.S. Senator and Representative. Jerry wrote a book entitled, *How You Can Help Clean Up America,* and offered it free upon request.

In a special message entitled, "It's Time to Clean Up America," Jerry issued a call for action. "You and I cannot change America alone. But together we can unite our efforts as concerned citizens to help return our country to a more stable condition. No nation can remain a strong local or international force with moral corruption deteriorating its foundations. We need your help in this effort. We can clean up America if we work together to make our voice heard in the land."

While the Clean Up America campaign garnered an immediate and enthusiastic response, it was not without its critics who questioned the legitimacy of a religious leader's involvement in public issues. Jerry answered this charge in a conversation with Tom Snyder on his nationally syndicated television show: "Homosexuality was a moral issue long before it became political. I am against abortion-on-demand because I consider it legalized murder. Today, it is political, but it was a moral issue. We as ministers cannot withdraw from conflict. I was against the giving up of the Panama Canal, but I didn't get involved because that was solely a political issue. However, homosexuality, abortion-on-demand, and pornography are issues which affect the lives of people and the moral posture of the nation. I have to lend my weight where I have the biblical right to do so."

Jerry told other critics, "When you begin to fight sin, you must expect to be criticized for your stand. If, however, you want to bring about a national revival, you must take your stand. There must be a realization of sin before a nation will seek God."

In addition to the issues involved in the two Clean Up

America campaigns, Jerry has spoken out against the Equal Rights Amendment and was largely responsible for its defeat in several states. He entered the battle against pari-mutuel betting when the polls revealed a two to one margin in its favor and turned the vote around so the final tally was fifty-three percent to forty-seven percent against legalized horse race betting.

Jerry has also voiced his opinion about IRS intervention in the attempt to legislate regulations that will control Christian schools. When Jerry takes a stand on an issue he must often debate his opposition on major television talk shows, where he has spoken forcefully and persuasively.

The membership of Thomas Road Baptist Church has always expected its leader to become directly involved with contemporary issues. Jerry has long taught his congregation the importance of Christian citizenship. "If a man is a committed Christian, he should also be a committed citizen. Christians, as individuals, should be meticulous in fulfilling their citizenship responsibilities. The local churches of any nation have the duty to act as the conscience of that nation."

In an interview on a Richmond radio station Jerry commented, "I allege that America for the main part was established as an alternative to European persecution and harassment of the free worship of God. America, more so than any nation, came into being with a Christian foundation. God has blessed this nation because we have followed this premise. But recently, we seem to have gone the other way. We as Christians have an obligation to do everything we can to keep America in a position where God has blessed us. For too long, liberals have succeeded in telling the world that religion and politics don't mix. The fact is that there is no arena in the world that needs an infusion of Bible Christianity like the political arena."

When the 1976 election returns were in, Jerry backed up his theme of responsible Christian citizenship by stating, "Jimmy Carter is now my President-elect, and he will have my respect and support. I will pray for him daily. But I will oppose him when he violates moral codes which in my opinion are in opposition to Scripture."

Jerry Falwell has not been afraid to take a publicly outspoken stance on controversial issues. He must do so, often at personal risk to himself and his family.

A small jet bounces through a thunderstorm as it turns east over the Long Beach breakwater. Inside, eight people are jammed together, waiting for the craft to touch down at Orange County Airport. From there the group will race by car to the local fairgrounds, where a crowd of several thousand has already gathered in anticipation of hearing Jerry Falwell speak against Proposition 6, a referendum that would clear the way for homosexuals to teach in all types of California schools. Jerry, who had flown out from Lynchburg earlier in the day, has just come from a similar rally at the San Diego Convention Center. Just before midnight he will drive to the Los Angeles International Airport for an all-night flight to Atlanta.

Jerry was called to help in California late in the fight against Proposition 6. Despite his intervention and the opposition of California's clergy, Proposition 6 did gain the approval of the state's electorate. It was very evident, however, that opponents had gained some ground. A similar measure in Dade County, Florida, failed, largely through the efforts of Jerry and his friend, Anita Bryant.

Jerry explained his opposition to Proposition 6 on Tom Snyder's *Tomorrow Show* on NBC. "I do not have anything against homosexuals. I believe they, like other persons who have a problem and need a change of life-style, require love and help; but at the same time, I am against homosexuality because the Bible teaches it is a perversion. If we allow homosexuality to be presented to the nation as an alternate life-style, it will not only have a corrupting influence upon the next generation of boys and girls, but it will bring the wrath of God down upon our nation. You cannot legislate holiness, but I think the church should be the conscience of America.''

Jerry views the question of homosexuality within the larger framework of the sanctity of the home. "I love homosexuals as souls for whom Christ died. Christ would say no to the homosexual life-style, but He would say yes to them as persons to be offered love and deliverance. We have a staff of Christian psychologists who deal with homosexuality and other moral problems. I am against the flaunting of a homosexual life-style before impressionable children. This is detrimental to the basic tenet of Christian society, the home.

"I firmly believe one is not born a homosexual but learns this through environment. Therefore, the home must be protected. At the center of the home is the father, who in subjection to the leadership of Christ, should be the dominant person. He should not be a dictator but should be a leader who sets the right example. The wife should be submissive to her husband, but she, of course, should be treated with love. The children should be taught by the parents not only in word, but also by the example of loving care and righteous living.''

One day in 1977 when Anita Bryant had reached a dead end in trying to enlist support for her cause, she picked up the telephone and called Jerry Falwell. "I told him how friends I had known and worked with all my life were giving me the cold shoulder. I was having trouble getting statements for a brochure. I was hearing a hemming and hawing you would not believe. I did not know Jerry personally at the time, but I was familiar with his ministry. My pastor at North West Baptist Church was one of Jerry's greatest admirers."

That initial conversation led to intensive contact. Jerry invited Bob Green, Anita's husband and manager, to Lynchburg. Soon after, both Anita and Bob came to Lynchburg. On a Saturday evening they attended a barbecue at the Falwell home. There the Greens asked Jerry if he could help them defeat an ordinance regarding the homosexual issue that was coming up for a vote in November. To their great shock and relief, Jerry told them he would come to Florida to hold a rally in their support, this despite the fact that some friends who had learned of his interest in the Greens' activities advised Jerry against becoming involved.

The following day Anita appeared to overflow crowds at the Thomas Road Baptist Church's three morning services, including an appearance on the *Old-Time Gospel Hour*. Jerry told his congregation that he would go to Florida to help Anita, that God had impressed him to do so. "We want the biggest place in Miami!" he said enthusiastically.

Ten days after the Green's visit to Lynchburg, ten thousand people filled the Miami Beach Convention Center, a feat no religious personality has been able to achieve since Billy Graham appeared there in the 1950s. Many people had to be turned away. When Bob and Anita entered the convention center, they were given a standing ovation. "Joy surged over my whole being," said Anita, "I was beside myself with emotion. I wanted to touch and embrace all those people, God's people. It turned out to be one of the most thrilling nights of our lives."

The message that came from Miami on June 7, 1977,

was one of victory. By a margin of more than two-to-one, citizens of Dade County had overwhelmingly voted against homosexuality as an acceptable life-style. Voter participation set a record.

Few people know that Jerry Falwell was extremely ill when he arrived at the convention center. Before the service, he was noticed to be perspiring heavily and seemed uncharacteristically tense. Anita, who did not know Jerry well at that point, had attributed his behavior to nervousness. She quickly revised this view when Jerry fainted just after the meeting. He was rushed by ambulance to a hospital and diagnosed as suffering from a kidney infection, a malady with which to this day he is periodically afflicted.

Some time later, when speaking about her stand, Anita Bryant commented. "Our unpopular stand regarding known practicing homosexuals' teaching in public and private schools thrust us into a dramatic and emotional struggle with those who opposed our convictions. We would not back down, even at the sacrifice of my career, because we knew we had to obey God. Our love for Almighty God, our love for God's Word, our love for our country, and our love for our children would not let us give up the fight.

"We read in Exodus 32:26, 'Who is on the LORD's side? let him come unto me.' Dr. Jerry Falwell was among the few preachers in this country who openly rallied to our cause. He obeyed God and unselfishly, sacrifically, and generously supported our efforts. He stood up and was counted at a crucial time. He never wavers in his firm conviction that sin must be faced and dealt with. When the church fails to uphold the biblical standards of righteousness, it ceases to be God's church. How we thank God for Dr. Jerry Falwell, a man who does not worry about the cost but who lives in obedience to God. He is a man who loves people everywhere and knows that God's love cannot be separated from His holiness. He is standing for God's absolutes and has risen in defense of the truth of God's Word.''

On December 3, 1978, just after the shooting of San Francisco's mayor and city supervisor, Jerry delivered one of his most outspoken *Old-Time Gospel Hour* sermons:

''Without question, San Francisco is undergoing a judgment from God today. I want to say that I am very much aware that there are some lovely Christian people in San Francisco. This ministry is supported by a lot of wonderful people in that city. I think it is probably one of the most beautiful cities in the world. I always look forward to seeing San Francisco. I am sorry that San Francisco has become, in the words of a former mayor of that city, an 'open city' where everybody, regardless of their sexual orientation, is welcome. This former official said, 'I'm glad that we have had a permissiveness here that has allowed people of these orientations to come here and do their own thing without intimidation, without reservation.' What he was really saying is that it doesn't matter to us what God thinks about it, we have endorsed what God has condemned whether He likes it or not.

''I have pity and real regard and compassion for the people in the city of San Francisco who are not a party to that sexual mutiny against God. But, at the same time, I would be derelict as a minister of the gospel if I failed to speak the conviction that is upon my heart. I believe that the preachers in San Francisco need to stand up tall and say the same thing. Romans chapter one is very clear, 'For the wrath of God is revealed from heaven against all ungodliness and unrighteousness of men, who hold the truth in unrighteousness.'

"Not long ago more than nine hundred people from the San Francisco area took their own lives in a suicide pact. They did this in Guyana under the influence of the Reverend Jim Jones. I believe that Jim Jones was Satan-possessed, that he had sold his soul to Satan. I believe the people, many of them well-intentioned I'm sure, had sold their souls to Jim Jones. I pity the families of those nine hundred people who now must live with that horrible thing forever.

"There is a vast difference between a cult and a Bible-believing group. If I were to ask this congregation today to do such a thing as Jim Jones asked of his followers, I would not have one volunteer. The allegiance of Bible-believing Christians is to the Christ of the Bible. If today I were to stop believing and practicing what is in the Bible, you people in this church would stop following me immediately. That is true of any Bible-believing, evangelical, fundamental Christian movement. If that is not true, then it is a cult. People who use events like that in Guyana as an opportunity to slam at Bible-believing Christianity are either uninformed or they are mad at God and Bible-believing Christianity."

This was not an easy message for Jerry Falwell to preach. He knew it would anger many people, but he spoke words he felt God had placed upon his heart to shake up many apathetic people across the nation. Jerry has never made the gospel "easy" in order to influence the nation's religious and political leaders by pandering to his audience or telling people what they want to hear. The old-time gospel that Jerry preaches is open to all by acceptance and faith, but he makes clear that salvation, although a free gift of God, involves a complete change in an individual's priorities.

Jerry continued his sermon: ''The people of San Francisco had better awaken to the fact that the judgment, the wrath that is falling upon the city, is of divine origin. The people of San Francisco had better rise up as people of God and say, 'We will have no more sin in our city. Let us call our city to repentance.' That had better happen in Lynchburg and in Los Angeles, in Philadelphia and in Kansas City, in Miami and in Jacksonville. That had better happen in every city in this land. Did you know that the homosexuals in San Francisco jokingly call Frisco 'Sodom and Gommorah'? This is a way of flaunting their arrogance in the face of almighty God.

''Christians should love homosexuals as they love all sinners, but we should call homosexuality what it is. It is perversion; it is reprobate; it is sin; it is abomination, and the only cure is the blood of Jesus Christ, God's own Son. Preachers in America hold the future of this nation in their hands. We had better say that adultery is just as wicked as homosexuality. The families of America are disintegrating. On prime-time national television we feature not only homosexuals, but divorce and broken homes. We feature unmarried people living together.

''To the three and four hundred thousand pastors in America, I say, 'Preach the Word of God unashamedly and fearlessly; call sin by its right name, and declare Jesus Christ and His death, burial, and resurrection, and His shed blood as the only atonement for sin. When you do this you can be assured that you're going to have all kinds of reprisals, repercussions, and pressures. They will come from inside your church, from inside your city, and if you preach on TV and radio, you will have it from the government and from everything high and low. Be willing to pay the price. Don't be afraid of the bitter attacks, threats, and vicious criticism you will get. Preach God's message if you bust. And as the Bible says, resist the devil and he will flee from you. We're supposed to be on the offense; so pastors, get your head out of the sand. If you've been a little bit afraid of what would happen to you and your security and your position, remember that God sent you to preach His gospel. Your first responsibility is to please God. If you don't please anybody else in the world but God, you can go to bed at night with a clear conscience; and if you please everybody else and don't please Him, you're a failure.'

"I'd like to say a word to the governors and the state legislators and to the congressmen and to all the members of the judiciary. I'd like to say to our President and to our Vice-President, to all the people in key places of leadership: 'According to the Bible, you are ministers of God, and you are ordained of God. Congressman, did you ever stop to think that you are an ordained minister? The Bible says that the powers that be are ordained of God. I believe that God is going to hold each of you men and women responsible for good or poor leadership. The people and their well-being and their future is in your hands politically. If you are going to be a good leader of men you have got to learn how to get before God and get direction from Him. 'If any of you lack wisdom,' James 1:5 says, 'let him ask of God, that giveth to all men liberally, and upbraideth not; and it shall be given him.' You can be the man of God, the woman of God, in that key place that God wants you to be. Let's start going back God's way.

"I want to say to all you editors, newspaper people, television people, and radio people: 'You have a tremendous potential to shake this country if you have the courage to do it. It could cost you your job, but there are a lot of things worse than being out of work. One of them is being in work and violating all the laws of God where you are.' There are a lot of people in key places who are going against their conscience, against God, against everything just to hold on to that paycheck every week. It would be better to be broke and in poverty, but have a clear conscience before God.

''I believe that America holds the key to world evangelization. What other nation in the world can give the gospel to the world except America? What other nation has the young people, the churches, the Bibles, the money, and the raw materials to evangelize the world? As a nation we must get back into the Bible, back into Christian families, and back into good, Bible-preaching, soul-winning churches.

''America needs a divine healing. Let us ask God for it. Revival begins when individuals repent of their sins and receive Jesus Christ as their Lord and Savior. That is why two thousand years ago Jesus died upon a cross, was buried, and rose again for the justification and salvation of a lost race. Wherever you are today, acknowledge if you are lost and need Jesus; will you bow your head and say, 'God have mercy upon me as a sinner; save me through the shed blood of your Son.' Will you invite Jesus Christ into your life right now? Please do it.''

Jerry Falwell is optimistic. He believes that America is going to have a spiritual awakening, that God will grant her one last reprieve. When God does this, it will be for the purpose of allowing His people one last opportunity to give the glorious gospel of Jesus Christ to the world with an intensity never practiced before. Meanwhile, Jerry Falwell will continue to work and pray, day and night with tears; he will continue to tell people with all the strength that is within him that Jesus Christ transforms lives. Then one day, either through death or through the Second Coming of Jesus Christ for His church, Jerry Falwell's life work will be completed and he will stand before the One who has given him everything worth living for. What a glorious day that will be!

7179